THE OLIVE TREE

Also by Arlene C. Stein

I LOVE YOU GOODBYE

THE OLIVE TREE

Arlene C. Stein

*"His branches shall spread,
and his beauty shall be as
the olive tree..."*
Hosea 14:7

S.I.M.A. PUBLISHERS Tamarac, Florida

Copyright ©1992 by Arlene C. Stein

All rights reserved.

No part of this book may be reproduced or transmitted in any form or by any means, electronic or mechanical, including photocopying, recording, or by any information storage and retrieval system, without permission in writing from the publisher.

Library of Congress Catalog Card Number 92-64465

ISBN 0-9634085-1-8 (Paper Cover)
ISBN 0-9634085-2-6 (Hard Cover)

Cover design by Connie Martino

Printed in the United States of America.

Dedication

*To my husband, Harry
And to our children,
Louis, Howard and Sherri,
On whom we depend to
Sustain our family heritage.
In memory of my beloved parents,
Mae and Moe Cohen.
Two lives that made a difference.*

*Special thanks to my loyal friends, especially
Frances Eckstein, Everett Gates,
Catherine Harris
Virginia Jackson, Maebelle Tanner,
and my husband, Harry Stein, whose
encouragement created a gentle,
steady breeze.*

Acknowledgments

One of the pleasurable benefits of working on *THE OLIVE TREE,* was the many contacts that were sought. New friendships were developed and past ones renewed.

Grateful appreciation goes to the following for their steadfast and generous cooperation in submission of photographs:

- Aurelia Lippman (Great-grandparents, Rayla and Meyer Grynbaum)
- Richard Floyd Plotka (Cecil Davis)
- Fran and Ron Pytko (Bessie Black's Delicatessen, Nookie's Delicatessen, New York Bakery, Bridge over Barge Canal at Sylvan Beach, Utica Free Academy, YMCA)
- Eleanor Cousins Scheidelman (Eastman Dormitory, Eastman Theatre)
- George and Bea Barth-White (John F. Hughes School, Munson-Williams Proctor Institute, New Century Club).

Special thanks to Dr. Eugene Fischer for providing background on paternal great-grandparents and grandparents. Also, to Aurelia Lippman and Samuel Greene for providing background on maternal great-grandparents and grandparents.

The Oneida County Historical Society was the most effective liaison for numerous details involved in publication of *THE OLIVE TREE.*

Sincere gratitude is expressed to Bono, Frank, Connie, Pat, Bill, Bob and Tom, whose genial natures and expertise were fundamental in producing *THE OLIVE TREE.*

Author's Note

Mama and Daddy always assumed that, eventually, this story would be told. Whenever she spoke about family affairs, Mama said with an air of confidence, "Someday, my dear, you will write *our* book."

It was something to which I gave little thought. Until, suddenly, one day, as though entranced, I began.

It was quite natural that I should write to Daddy, since Mama told us from early childhood on, that he was our favorite. However, one must readily agree that as I write to *Dearest Daddy,* the rich and beautiful memories of Mama are ever present.

Of one thing I remain certain. Mama's love was special. Our family was unique. Those days will always be recalled with love as I am guided by some hidden power to write this collection of short stories as a tribute to Mae and Moe Cohen.

Most names in THE OLIVE TREE are not fictitious, but several have been changed to protect the privacy of individuals.

Contents

The Beginning 1
Aunt Marian 5
Lucky Number Seven 9
Leslie Avenue 15
The High Holy Days 21
Succoth and Simchat Torah Night 25
Simchat Torah Joy and Sorrow 29
The Dawn 33
A Day On The Road 39
At The Top Of The Hill 45
Shabat 55
Harriet and Mac 63
Alarm Clock A Cappella 71
Eyes Down and Watch Your Numbers 77
Erwin's Home Decorators 83
Beloved Maestro 91
Girl Scout Cookies 99
Sharing Traditions 105
Chanukah, Purim and Passover 111
Pastrami On Rye and Apple Strudel 123
Election Day 129
Singing Praises 135
Sweet Sixteen 143
The Summer I Learned to Drive 149
The Road Not Taken 155
Union Station 161
The Engagement Gift 167
All The Days 173

Mama's Showers	179
Our Wedding	185
Mama's Driving Lessons	191
Chicken Soup and Tsihmes	197
The Brihs	203
Louise and Butter-Puff	207
The Day We Headed South	213
Turn Around	221
The Attic	225
The Minyan	231
Bar Mitzvahs	237
Sudden Death and Broken Ties	241
Precious Jewels Priceless Flashback	247
Sunshine and Sorrow	255
The Cycle of Life	259
Where Have All The Cousins Gone?	263
Concerts and Recitals	269
Rabbi Lazer	273
Dreams	279
Epilogue	283

"Thy wife shall be as a fruitful vine, in the innermost parts of thy house; Thy children like olive plants, round about thy tables."
Psalms 128:3

Our PATERNAL GREAT-GRANDPARENTS, MEYER (Meyer ha Kohen) and IDA (Chayeh) COHEN, evidently brought forth their five offspring in Novidvor, in the state of Vilna, country of Russia.

Their five children were Mordechai Zev, Israel, Solomon, Joseph and one daughter, Sarah Cohen Berger.

Meyer Cohen died before the families came to the United States. Ida Cohen, it is believed, lived until her mid-ninetieth years and died in Utica, New York.

Our PATERNAL GREAT GRANDMOTHER, IDA COHEN

PARENTS OF MAX COHEN

Our PATERNAL GREAT GRANDFATHER, MEYER COHEN

Our PATERNAL GRANDPARENTS, MAX (Mordechai Zev ben Meyer ha Kohen) and IDA (Hades bas Yisrael) COHEN met when he went to visit his brother, Solomon in Vashidishach, a city of five hundred families, approximately two hundred of whom were Jewish.

They were married about three months later in January 1895.

Max Cohen was born in January 1870 in Novidvor, a city of approximately one hundred twenty families, of which about seventy-five were Jewish. He was privately taught by a "Rebbe" and at the age of thirteen was apprenticed to a shoemaker in Novidvor. He worked there for three years, then went to Vilne where he lived for nine years, earning the approximate equivalent of five to six dollars per week. He then returned to Novidvor to open his own shop and was thereafter married.

Max and Ida's children and their approximate birth dates are as follows:
    Israel Herman (January 1896)
    Harry (April 1897)
    Sarah (October 1899)
    Moses (November 1901)
    Anna (1903)
    Male child (1905 - died when one year old)
    Mae (1906)
    Leah (June 1908)
    Esther (August-September 1909)
    Male twin who died at four months
    Mary (Marian) (June 1914)

In February 1909, Max Cohen left Russia and traveled to Hamburg, Germany where he took a boat, Graf Walderse, to the United States. After a journey of seventeen days, he arrived at Ellis Island in April 1909 and went directly to Utica, New York.

No history remains of Ida Cohen before her marriage to Max. It is believed that she was orphaned at an early age. Her maiden family name was Koran.

Our PATERNAL Grandparents: Mordechai Zev Cohen and Hades bas Yisrael Koran.
MAX and IDA COHEN.

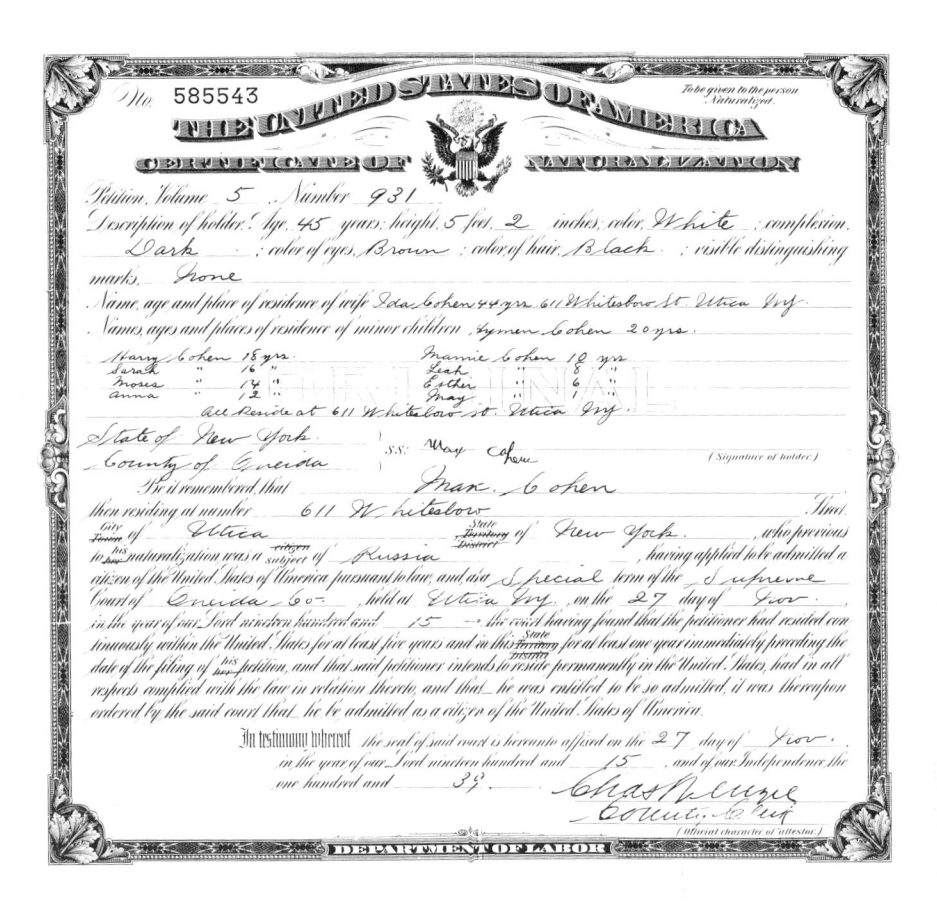

Certificate of Naturalization
Ida and Max Cohen
and nine children
(Marian, the ninth child,
was born in the United States.)

Family of Ida and Max Cohen, Circa 1923

1st Row, L. to R.: Herman, (wife) Edith, Marian (front), Max and Ida (parents).
Back Row, L. to R.: Mae, Frances, (wife of Harry, Leah, Esther (foreground), Morris, (husband of Anna, Sam, (husband of Sarah, Son, Milton (chair) and Moses.

Our MATERNAL GREAT-GRANDPARENTS, MEYER and RAYLA GRYNBAUM, presumably brought forth their offspring in Drubnin, a village in Russia Poland. The original spelling of Grynbaum, according to legend, was changed by officials at Ellis Island, when various members of the family came to the United States, and assumed the spelling of Grinbaum or Greenbaum. Some members altered the name to Greene.

The siblings were Shmuel Moishe, Hershel, Aaron and Levi (Louie). Aaron had a twin sister who died at birth.

Meyer and Rayla never came to the United States. Their dates of birth and death are not known.

MATERNAL GREAT-GRANDPARENTS
MEYER & RAYLA GRYNBAUM

Our MATERNAL GRANDPARENTS, AARON and SARAH FREIDEL GREENBAUM, apparently had what was considered an arranged marriage and lived in Drubnin, Poland, sometime around 1900.

In 1904, Aaron Greenbaum, the son of our MATERNAL GREAT-GRANDPARENTS, MEYER AND RAYLA GRYNBAUM, traveled by ship to the United States, landed at Ellis Island, and came directly to Utica, New York and remained with a first cousin by the family name of Pfeffer. After one year, he sent for his wife and child.

Sarah Freidel Jacobs Greenbaum, daughter of our MATERNAL GRANDPARENTS, SHIMSHE YUNKOV and GREAT BUBBE JACOBS, (possibly Channah) had four sisters and two brothers, all of whom settled in New York State with the exception of Etta, who settled in Chicago. The siblings were Bayla, Raisel, Etta, Molly, Itzchak and Abram.

Although their father, Shimshe Yunkov, must have died in Europe, the mother lived with one or another of her daughters in New York City, where she later expired at the age of 90. It is told that when she died, her daughter, Sarah Freidel, living in poverty in Utica, had no means with which to attend her mother's funeral. And so she sat by the window that day, surrounded by grievous wretchedness, and there she wept.

Aaron and Sarah Freidel's children and their birth dates are as follows:
   Shoshe Miriam (December 9, 1903. Before research, the date was thought to be the 20th of December. It was on this date that her birthday was celebrated throughout her life.)
   Yunkov Meyer (May 18, 1907)
   Rayla (January 18, 1913)

Sarah Freidel and daughter, Shoshe Miriam, came to the United States in 1905. They remained with the Pfeffer family until Aaron found them a place to live.

Both Shoshe Miriam and her brother, Yunkov Meyer, were named after their maternal and paternal grandfathers.

After surviving a difficult birth with their son, Sarah Freidel was advised not to have more children. However, nearly six years later, she gave birth to a third child, Rayla. The three children were raised in Utica as Mamie, Yunk and Aurelia Greenbaum.

Our MATERNAL Grandparents: Aaron Greenbaum and Sarah Freidel Jacobs.
AARON and SARAH GREENBAUM.

They had three children: Shoshe Miriam (Mamie), Jacob Meyer, Aurelia

In 1905, at the age of two, Shoshe Miriam Greenbaum, born in Drubnin, Poland, traveled to the United States with her mother. Her father had come the year before and was living with cousins as he tried to establish a life for his family. Her brother, Yunk (Jacob Meyer) and sister, Aurelia, were born in Utica where the family settled. The family lived in poverty during their entire childhood. Upon graduation from Utica Free Academy, Shoshe Miriam, whose name later evolved to Mamie, then Mae, yearned to continue with a college education and become a teacher. However, circumstances forced her to give up her desire and instead, help support the family.

While employed as a bookkeeper for the Cohen business, she began to keep company with one of the young men, Moses, who would later become her husband.

Moses Cohen, the third son and fourth child of Max and Ida Cohen, was born in Novidvor, somewheres in the vicinity of Vilne, Lieder Uhyest, Astrin and Vashidishach. When he was very young, no more than six years old, his parents sent him to Vashidishach by horse and wagon, to study with a "Rebbe" and live with strangers.

Since their father was in the United States with the three older siblings, Moses was entrusted with the care of the remainder of the family who remained behind. In 1913, when he was somewheres between twelve and thirteen years old, Moe helped his mother and remaining four children make the journey by ship to the United States, where they landed at Ellis Island.

Moe had to immediately assist his father and older siblings in making a living. However, he found time and energy to attend night school, where he quickly learned to speak English.

He carried a pack on his back and went from door to door selling novelty items. And it was thus that he proceeded from boyhood to manhood.

Mae and Moe Cohen were the parents of two sons and a daughter, Herbert, Arlene and Eugene.

This is our Mama,
Shoshe Miriam Greenbaum who
became the wife of Moses Cohen
on March 30, 1930.

This is our Daddy,
Moses Cohen.

These two photographs were presumably taken shortly before their marriage, circa 1930.

Certificate of Marriage

This is to Certify that

On the _1_ day of the week, the _1_ day of the month _Nison_ in the year 56_90_, A. M., corresponding to the _30_ of _March_ _1930_, the holy Covenant of Marriage was entered into, in _Syracuse_ between the Bridegroom _Moe Cohen_ and his Bride _Mae Greenbaum_.

The said Bridegroom made the following declaration to his Bride: "Be thou my wife according to the law of Moses and of Israel. I faithfully promise that I will be a true husband unto thee. I will honor and cherish thee; I will work for thee, I will protect and support thee, and will provide all that is necessary for thy due sustenance, even as it becomes a Jewish husband to do. I also take upon myself all such further obligations for thy maintenance, as are prescribed by our religious statute."

And the said Bride has plighted her troth unto him in affection and sincerity, and has thus taken upon herself the fulfilment of all the duties incumbent upon a Jewish wife.

This Covenant of Marriage was duly executed and witnessed this day according to the usage of Israel.

Witnesses: _Harry Abram_
Herman Revitz

**Mama and Daddy's
Wedding Certificate**

בס״ד

כתובת בית הלל

בסימן טוב ומזל טוב

באחד בשבת אחד לחדש אלול שנת חמשת אלפים ושש
מאות ותרפ״ק לבריאת עולם למנין שאנו
מונין כאן בציור סיטיע״ל במדינת אמעריקא הצפונית איך
החתן אשר בר׳ ארדסי הכהן
אמר לה להדא בתולתא ליבא אדיס
בת ר׳ מהרן הוי לי לאנתתי כדת משה
וישראל ואנא אפלח ואוקיר ואיזון ואפרנס יתיכי ליכי כהלכות גוברין יהודאין דפלחין
ומוקרין וזנין ומפרנסין לנשיהון בקושטא ויהיבנא ליכי מהר בתולתיך
כסף זוזי מאתן דחזי ליכי מדאורייתא ומזונייכי וכסותייכי
וסיפוקיכי ומיעל לותיכי כאורח כל ארעא וצביאת מרת אדיס
בתולתא דא והות לה לאנתו ודין נדוניא דהנעלת לה מבי בכסף
בין בדהב בין בתכשיטין במאני דלבושא בשמושי דירה ובשמושי דערסא הכל קבל עליו
חתן דנן אסלא וקוקים כסף צרוף וצבי
חתן דנן והוסיף לה מן דיליה עוד אסלא זקוקים כסף צרוף אחרים כנגדן סך הכל
זקוקים כסף צרוף וכך אמר חתן דנן אחריות שטר כתובתא
דא נדוניא הן ותוספתא דא קבלית עלי ועל ירתי בתראי להתפרע מכל שפר ארג נכסין
וקנינין דאית לי תחות כל שמיא דקנאי ודעתיד אנא למקנא. נכסין דאית להון אחריות ודלית
להון אחריות כלהון יהון אחראין וערבאין לפרוע מנהון שטר כתובתא דא נדוניא דן ותוספתא
דא מנאי ואפילו מן גלימא דעל כתפאי בחיי ובתר חיי מן יומא דנן ולעלם ואחריות שטר
כתובתא דא נדוניא דן ותוספתא דא קבל עליו אסלא חתן דנן כחומר
כל שטרי כתובות ותוספתות דנהגין בבנות ישראל העשויין כתקון חכמינו זכרם לברכה דלא
כאסמכתא ודלא כטופסי דשטרי וקנינא מן אסלא בר׳ ארדסי הכהן
חתן דנן למרת אדיס בתולתא בת ר׳ מהרן בחפצא
דא על כל הא דכתיב ומפרש לעיל במנא דכשר למקניא בה.

והכ״ל שריר וקים.

נאום _____
נאום _____

Certificate of Naturalization
Mamie Greenbaum

Utica Free Academy

UTICA, NEW YORK

Be it known that *Mamie S. Greenbaum*, having satisfactorily completed a four years course is hereby entitled to this

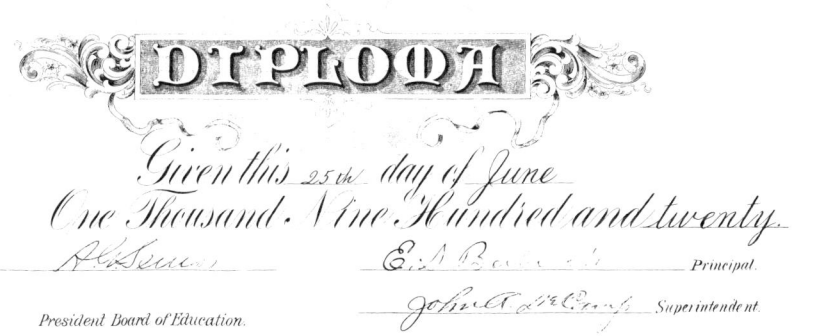

DIPLOMA

Given this 25th day of June One Thousand Nine Hundred and twenty.

_____ President Board of Education.

_____ Principal.

_____ Superintendent.

Mama's High School Diploma

Mama Before Marriage
Circa 1925 - 1929

Mama Circa 1940

The Beginning

"... for the tribes of the children of Israel shall cleave each one to its own inheritance."
Numbers 36:9

Dearest Daddy,

Today, for no particular reason, I tuned in television and found myself watching *Little House On The Prairie*. The small town was about to celebrate United States Centennial 1876.

Community members, one by one, were losing faith as they met with the town tax collector for annual assessment. One family, immigrants from Russia, having purchased land, unaware of responsibility for seven years' back taxes, were forced to leave the property when they could not meet the obligation. Even so, the story ended in beautiful tribute to these United States by the Russian immigrant father. He praised our country for the freedom it provides, a stirring reminder to count our blessings.

With sudden perceptiveness, I imagined a thirteen year old boy who came to this country in 1913, head of part of his family. The father had arrived in the United States several years earlier, from the small village of Novidvor, Russia. He left his wife and eight children behind. His sister, Sarah, brothers Joseph and Azar, already settled in Utica, New York with their families, took him under their care.

Working in a shoemaker shop, he soon became enterprising enough to assume his own business as a cobbler. His frugality turned pennies into dollars. Within four years, he sent for Herman and Harry, the two older sons. The boys helped their father in his shop. A short time later, enough money was saved to send for Sarah, the oldest daughter.

Time quickly passed. Each day, the father, Max, his two sons and daughter worked from dawn to dusk, sewing, mending, cobbling. Saving pennies, dimes, dollars. Their fervent task ever before their eyes, compelled them to toil beyond physical endurance. Their mother, younger brother and four sisters must come to America as soon as possible. Finally, there was enough money and tickets were purchased.

The boy, assuming responsibility with solemn dignity and maturity well beyond his thirteen years, headed the journey huddled with family members on a freighter that would take them to America, the land of opportunity. The presumably first class tickets actually meant first class cellar or steerage. Although the family suffered from poverty, cleanliness had been their custom

Thrown into squalorous conditions, they lay in silence, trying to comfort one another. During the pitiful voyage, food consisted solely of a type of herring into whose liquid morsels of bread were dipped.

Weeks later, approaching Ellis Island, they were speechless as they glanced up and saw her magnificent beauty and stature. But the words were undistinguishable to their foreign tongue. *Give me your tired, your poor, your huddled masses yearning to breathe free.* The Statue of Liberty. America . . . America.

In years to follow, this serious-minded boy would become the father of three children. First generation born in these United States. Thank you, Daddy, for giving us this gift. The gift of life in a free country.

Aunt Marian

*"For this child I prayed;
and the Lord hath given me
my petition which I asked
of him . . ."*
  I. Samuel 1:27

Dearest Daddy,

When you came to this country with your mother and four sisters, Buba and Zeda, our grandparents, already had eight living children. Esther, the youngest, had survived a twin brother. Somewhere along the line, another boy had died in early childhood.

Buba and Zeda's eight living children were rapidly maturing as a result of their difficult life style. They were helping their parents survive. First in the old country, now, in America.

One day, a family member suddenly noticed that Buba appeared to be expecting another child. Their dwelling place was already overcrowded. The three boys, accustomed to sleeping in one double bed, were inwardly relieved that Herman, the oldest, was contemplating marriage. Perhaps he would soon move out and leave a bit of breathing space.

The daughters were overcome with resentment. Sore fingers and red hands were not unusual as each took their turn at scrubbing laundry on a board which stood in a large tub on the kitchen floor. Would this tedious life never end? What right did their mother have to bring another mouth into this world?

One day, several months later, their mother experienced the usual pains of labor. The midwife came and helped deliver the infant, another daughter.

Buba and Zeda gazed in anguish at their other children. The sanctity of life which they cherished was written on their faces. A sudden hush came over the household. Marian, their sixth daughter and ninth living child, was here to stay.

Lucky Number Seven

*"To every thing there is a season,
and a time to every purpose
under the heaven;
A time to be born . . ."*
  Ecclesiastes 3:1-2

Dearest Daddy,

That hot summer day in 1935 caused you and Mama tears of anxiety before I made my appearance. Cousins were visiting. In a moment of non-concern, while leaving to visit other relatives for the day, they left their automobile parked behind yours in the driveway. Evidently, I decided to give Mama no warning in anticipation of my entrance into the world.

She began to experience pangs of approaching childbirth. Rushing towards the door, you both suddenly realized the lack of transportation. Moments seemed endless as you waited for a taxi to arrive. On the way to the hospital, the cab driver helped to reassure Mama that she would arrive in time. Her cries of doubt as the driver defied customary rules of driver etiquette, threw you into helpless frustration. Bravely holding her hand, you attempted to console her.

Dr. Sloan, Mama's physician, was away that Fourth of July holiday weekend and Mama was further annoyed by his absence. There was little time, however, for her to voice concern. In very few moments I began taking my place in your lives. Soon, you were blessed with a baby girl to become the sister of Herbert Erwin, big brother, who was two years and eight months my senior. I was given the Hebrew name of Esther and named after my Zeda, Aaron, whom I would never meet. Mama's father had died the preceding year. According to tradition, a newborn child was named after a deceased loved one. Whether male or female, the name was usually matched as closely as possible.

On the seventh day of the seventh month of the year, at seven minutes past seven a.m., weighing seven pounds thirteen ounces, I was born into this world. In likeness to that young cartoon character known to promenade with his coverlet, the number seven ultimately became my security blanket. No matter what the situation, I reckoned with it in terms of my lucky number. Life invariably allowed me to make choices involving my symbol of opportune.

Perhaps the fact that I was born on Sunday made my birthday each year seem like a special holiday. Possibly, it was merely considered a continuation of spectacular Fourth of July festivities. Most of my classmates thought that celebration of their birthdays during the school season were special events. I secretly thanked heaven that my birthday occurred on a wonderful summer day with no thoughts of school or studies. Being the only daughter also had advantages where birthdays were concerned. Mama expended femininely inclined energy on me. I had no competition.

One could readily acquire a complex or be amused by songs that were written the year of my birth. Three celebrated hits, popular this very day, were, *I Got Plenty O Nothin'*, *It Ain't Necessarily So,* and *Just One Of Those Things*.

Astrologically speaking, I have long assumed my musical aspirations were acquired as much by the Cancer sign under which I was born, as from biological inheritance. My birthday is shared with Gustav Mahler and Gian Carlo Menotti, two of the world's greatest composers. Although our signs differ, I can give humble recognition to being born the same year as one of the world's greatest tenors, the inestimable Pavarotti.

Genetically speaking, whenever asked about our family's musical background, I was wont to reply that my father used his beautiful voice for cantorial chanting, my Uncle Herman was a violinist of considerable achievement, Aunt Esther extoled pianistic virtue as a conservatory graduate, and Aunt Marian was, indeed, a comely soprano. Surely, it was pre-destined that a child born into such a family, given seven for her lucky number, would experience life's blessings.

Leslie Avenue

*"The lines are fallen unto me in pleasant places;
Yea, I have a goodly heritage."*
　　Psalms 16:6

Dearest Daddy,

Surely, it was pre-destined. The day when I'd return to our childhood home with you and Mama no longer at my side. It was as though a time machine button were pressed and I was spun into a millenium where one could feel the sparks and powerful surge of lifelong dreams that had already come and gone.

I was nearing my fourth year of life that spring day when you and Mama, big brother and I moved into our new home. I remember slipping quietly downstairs to the basement, so mysterious and haunting to my young mind. A coal bin heaped to the ceiling lay in wait. Soon, you embarked for the next few years on the chore of shoveling coal into the large furnace each night when you returned from peddling on the road.

Heavy cans of ashes were carried up those stairs as we watched our Daddy endure this tiresome burden. Young scoundrels who lived up the street would sneakily watch for the arrival each night of the ash cans. Soon after you sat down to relax, sounds could be heard as the cans were thrown upside down into a mountain of snow. One night, when your patience had reached its peak, you hurried outside and chased these monstrous characters down the avenue, around the block, up the hill, and to their home. Clutching them by their collars, you delivered them to their father. It was the last time we watched you suffer from strewn ashes.

Mama's green and cream colored washing machine

was located in the basement beside the gray iron wash tubs. There she stood each day, wringing the family's clothing through the hand wringer. Up and down, back and forth she climbed as each wash cycle was completed between her cleaning and cooking. It was many years later that Mama's laundry days became easier with the addition of a modern washer and dryer to our home. How pleasurable it was to load a machine and return forty minutes later to transfer clean laundry from washer to dryer.

During those early days, after using the hand wringer, Mama neatly folded the wet laundry and piled it high into the large wicker basket. She carried it upstairs to the sun room. No matter how cold the day, she opened the window and carefully maneuvered the pully clothesline, hanging each article with large wooden clothes pins. When the line was full, down came the window. Taking one step to the right, Mama stood at the adjoining window, opened it, swung herself into position and filled a second clothesline with the family bedding, linens and clothing. On winter days, it was questionable as to how well everything dried. Most articles were stiff as boards, some dripping with icycles. But, oh, so fresh and clean smelling.

Mama was fussy and meticulous as she kept house. Everything must shine. Each dinner must be a work of art fit for any cuisine contest the world over. Even Mama's laundry had to be soft and white, starched and ironed, folded to perfection. A large white enamel pan was often seen sitting on the stove. In it was Mama's homemade starch which she stirred with a big wooden spoon before dipping clothing or linens into the pan. Piece by piece, each item was starched before ironing. Whether it be an exquisite linen table cloth, a brightly colored school dress or merely a simple kitchen towel, each was deemed equally important in Mama's eyes and ironed with the same amount of care.

Towards the end of April, when the days began to feel warm, you and Mama chose one Sunday to complete the task of washing down the porch, gathering up the long straw rug from the basement, and dragging the heavy furniture to the porch. We thrilled to the sight of the heavy iron glider with its bright floral cushions. We'd sit for hours, either reading or playing with paper dolls as we swung back and forth, back and forth, shaded by the green striped awnings on the side and front of the porch. Facing the glider were two sturdy metal chairs, cool, straight-backed and comfortable, where you and Mama sat in the evenings.

Each afternoon, late in the day, when Mama did not work in the store, she dressed for dinner and came outside. There she sat, on the porch with her knitting. Mama was an absolute expert. An artist. She never produced an article with an imperfection. Often, she was seen counting stitches or re-doing a small piece in which an error had been made. One summer, she decided it was time I learned to knit. She bought a little red spool with four tiny hooks at the top. Somehow, I was to twist and turn a piece of yarn around those hooks, lower it to the inside of the spool where a braided piece gathered inches into a long tail. I was left-handed and Mama was very understanding. She had begun school as a left-hander and was made to use her right hand. She had been treated badly as a child and determined that I would continue in life as a lefty. Somewheres between Mama's right hand and my left, we lost ourselves and soon gave up. Embroidery was next. Mama helped me with a charming sampler that said, *For These We Give Thanks*. It still decorates our table each Shabat, covering a challah, the Sabbath loaf. The summer days ended too quickly. Soon, the porch was bare.

The year is 1940. The house on Leslie Avenue, of ample room size, cozily decorated and handsomely furnished, holds within it symbols of a peaceful and happy family. It permeates with love and warmth. Mama's cooking arouses feelings of excitement as the children enter her kitchen. One sees forever a picture of her at the stove with its high legs. It matches exactly, the washing machine with colors of cream and green sitting in the basement. Outside, the snow is falling as it becomes dark and overcome with dreariness of winter. It is so wonderful to be in the confines of home.

The High Holy Days

*"Train up a child in the way he should go,
and even when he is old, he will not depart from it."*
Proverbs 22:6

Dearest Daddy,

At first, I was apprehensive. An intense feeling of despair, knowing you would not be with us for Rosh Hashonah or Yom Kippur. When beloved Mama died two years earlier, I consoled myself with the fact that at least we still had Daddy.

Oh, the grief one feels with that final loss of both parents. When we know for certain that we are the oldest living generation. The sudden realization that our children, God willing, will survive us. That we have survived our parents.

Memories returned day after day with continuous flow of tears. I wondered how many of Mama's pots could be filled with my tears. Awakened by morning sunshine, my luminous thoughts were suddenly overtaken by a childhood remembrance. The tears would commence.

So clear was my vision of a small child dressed in holiday finery walking hurriedly behind her father on a railroad track without end. The ties continued mile after mile. Only the child and her father. Periodically, he turned around, glancing quickly to reassure himself of her presence.

The synagogue or shul as it was called, was reminiscent of those in the shtetels, those small towns in Europe. Its balcony, for women only, was live with gossip of the day. Yosel's heart attack *erev* or preceding Rosh Hashonah. Molly's engagement to Chaim broken yesterday. Disgrace to their families. On and on they babbled while their husbands prayed dutifully on the bimah, the alter below. They held their prayer books as they talked. Only the kaddish for their eternally resting loved ones would serve to remind them of where they were. The elderly European women seemed to consider the formality of prayer obligatory to their husbands rather than themselves.

The little girl dutifully remained silent, waiting for her mother to arrive. Awhile later, a lady dressed in elegance, hat of softly blended feathers, sat down beside the small child. Patting her hand, the mother tenderly smiled at her child and handed her a brown bag containing a jelly sandwich, shiny red apple, cookies and grapes. Hopefully, the child's hunger would be quenched until sundown tonight.

Today was that day of days, Yom Kippur, Day of Atonement, when grown-ups refrained from food and drink for more than twenty-four hours. They would not return home until very late. The little girl knew well the solemnity of this holy day. Her parents were to her, the holiest of holies.

Her mother cooked delicious meals for them and kept a strictly kosher home. Tonight's meal, including boiled potatoes, had been prepared yesterday, before the holiday began. Supper would be on the table minutes after their arrival home. The family car had taken them to shul before sundown last night and was parked nearby so they could drive home after dark, when services ended.

Her big brother who had arrived with their mother, sat with father. She could barely see her Daddy and brother when she peered through the balcony railing. They seemed so far away on the floor below. There he was. Her Daddy. She recognized him even from his back. And the tallit. The prayer shawl that he wore.

Succoth and Simchat Torah Night

"Let the children of Zion be joyful in their King.
Let them praise His name in the dance . . ."
  Psalms 149:2-3

Dearest Daddy,

Tomorrow will usher in Succoth, when Jews throughout the world celebrate the harvest season. Instinctively, I found myself at farmers' market, staring at barrels of fruit. Shiny red apples, large seedless grapes, red and green bartlet pears. A pomegranate caught my eye. How incomplete the large fruit bowl would be without this thick skinned reddish fruit of many seeds.

Gazing at an enormous red apple, I met the reflection of a young girl holding a brightly decorated paper flag. Fastened securely on top of the wooden flag stick, was a huge red apple. The little girl was surrounded by dozens of children with flags, prepared to march around the room when the signal would be given.

It was Simchat Torah night. Festival of Torah Joy. Children and parents alike had a glow on their faces. An air of ecstacy, pure happiness filled the shul. The child was overcome with awe. An air of expectation was evident in facial expressions of her parents and their friends.

This was the one holy day of the year when men allowed themselves the freedom of frivolity as they danced and sang, taking turns carrying the Torahs. The girl's mother sat quietly with a smile, watching with pleasure as her husband took his turn singing and davening with the other men.

Oh, night of nights. Wonder of wonders. The young girl was so happy to be alive, stirred by her Jewish roots. Thankful to have been born to this beautiful couple. Her Mom and Dad. Simchat Torah. A very special night in their lives.

Simchat Torah Joy and Sorrow

"One generation passeth away and another generation cometh: but the earth abideth for ever."
Ecclesiastes 1:4

Dearest Daddy,

As the days spew forth since you left us, it has become increasingly difficult to recall your unique voice. The power and beauty behind it as you davened and chanted services for hundreds of congregants during your lifetime. Oh, that you were here now to glorify our Simchat Torah.

During the past decades, we have been blessed with the invention of that small, but miraculous machine, the tape recorder. Whatever possessed me one morning when I decided to carry this convenient device to services in our little shul, Anshe Emet? I knew it was not the proper thing to do, but I also knew the liberal minds of our congregants would not prevent me from acting against orthodox principles.

You were leading the service. I suppose, deep in my subconscious mind, I was preparing for that someday when I should long to hear your voice. Now, I am spiritually uplifted as I listen to you conducting that Simchat Torah service of years ago. What a relief, to hear your splendid voice once more as you chant the poetic mysticism of our ancestors.

Suddenly, I see before me the young girl with dark plaided braids, brightly colored silk ribbons neatly placed on each side of her head. She stares at her father on the bimah below, gazing in awe as his calm, but radiant voice stirs the congregation. Soon, it will be time to join the adults as they celebrate this momentous festival.

At conclusion of the service, the small child is joined

by her father and brother. The children follow his quick step, each taking the hand he offers. His parents, their Buba and Zeda, live only minutes from the synagogue, but were too worn and tired to come to shul this evening.

The children and their father are warmly greeted. Smells of delicious baked goods permeate the house. They know that Buba will soon have sponge cake and glasses of milk on the table.

Father and his parents converse in Yiddish as is their custom. The children are secretly pleased, for they comprehend every word. For some mysterious reason, their senses told them at a very early age that Yiddish was the language of understanding. It amuses them to know that their parents and family members often speak in their secret language to prevent young ears from hearing certain things. What would they think, were they to discover the children understood every word spoken?

As they speak, Buba and Zeda frequently glance at their two grandchildren in admiration. Soon, the visit is over and the loved ones embrace with fondness.

The telephone rings in the very next hours of early morning, still in darkness. The little girl is aroused from her sleep. Moments later, her brother enters the room. With terror in his voice and cries of anguish, he moans, *"Buba has died. She's died. Our Buba has died."*

The Dawn

". . . and to enjoy pleasure for all his labour, wherein he laboureth under the sun, all the days of his life which God hath given him; for this is his portion."
Ecclesiastes 5:17

Dearest Daddy,

How deeply treasured are memories of our tiny summer cottage on the lake. It began in the very early years of your marriage, when Herb, our big brother, was a baby. Each summer, you and Mama rented the same little abode at Sylvan Beach, where, for several blocks up and down the beach, Mama's cousins also came to stay with their children.

During the week, children and their mothers busily engaged in all sorts of activities while the daddies remained in the city to work. Towards the weekend, we gathered in anticipation as one by one, our fathers made their way to the beach to spend a few days with their families.

We were never aware that you rented *The Dawn*. We thought it was our summer home. The sun room, with its three walls of windows, faced the lake. A breakfast nook with bay window held the round wooden table and chairs from where we viewed our neighbors while we ate. The only bedroom had a double bed. In the sun room was a colorful couch that opened into another bed.

During the week, while you were gone, I slept with Mama. We'd lie there huddled in darkness, listening to eerie sounds of the lake outside our window. We were so relieved when you arrived each week to spend those few days. Somehow, the sounds of night were never so scary when Daddy was there. You were our strength. Our protector. Moreover, when Daddy came, we could go to the Midway.

The Midway, perhaps half a mile or less from the cottage, held all sorts of inviting things. From the distance, one could see lights on the ferris wheel. Music from the merry-go-round enchanted us, but we were overwhelmed by the vast colorful animation. We begged to go on the rides. Then, Daddy finally had to accompany us.

My bravery never withstood the ferris wheel. Only once, did I attempt it. Then, the attendant had to stop the wheel midst my screams, and allow me to disembark. The live ponies lured me, though I shook with fear the entire time I rode. Yet, the thrill and excitement seemed to make it all worthwhile.

Strange smells pervaded the air as we begged for something to eat. The smell of the non-kosher hot dog was foreign to our nostrils. French-fried potatoes were a mystery, as were cotton candy and candied apples that passersby held on a stick. If endowed with incredible luck, and had we not teased too much, we were treated to an ice cream cone towards the end of the evening. This was sheer happiness as we sauntered slowly back to the cottage. What a treat. What a night. How fortunate. We were blessed with great wealth, without doubt, the luckiest children on earth.

Owners of *The Dawn,* the Freyburgers, lived directly across the street in a larger year-round house. Their son, Bill, was in charge of removing our garbage and providing ice for the ice box. Refrigeration was not commonly available in lakefront summer cottages. Bill came two or three times during the week. Although I was quite small, he was probably very tall. I remember hiding behind Mama each time he came, staring high into the air at this giant figure. His booming laughter was even more frightful. Years later, I was assured of his immensity when we heard that Bill had become a state trooper.

Although, at the time, I was too young to realize it, we stayed at *The Dawn* each summer during the month of July. For this reason, Fourth of July followed three days later by my birthday, was always celebrated at *The Dawn*. What a glorious place to celebrate one's birthday. The memories are vivid!

Mama worked for two days on her special three-layer cake. She knew how to create things in one manner. Perfection. The cake, frosted in white, was decorated with exquisite pink and yellow flowers with green leaves.

Mama's cakes were truly works of art. We were sent outside to play. We built sandcastles on the beach in front of the cottage. My birthday cake was to be a secret. Isn't it strange that I have little recollection of most presents received? Yet, mental images of those beautiful birthday cakes made by Mama are as real as the day they were baked.

The Dawn. Even its name causes one to remember the beauty and magnificence of those early days. They remain forever imbedded in our minds as we recall those purely delightful moments of our childhood.

A Day on the Road

*"A man shall be satisfied with good by the fruit of his mouth,
And the doings of a man's hands shall be rendered unto him."*
    Proverbs 12:14

Dearest Daddy,

One morning, as you prepared to leave, I summoned up courage to ask if I might spend the day with you on the road. Overwhelmed by your affirmative reply, I hurried to dress. With our goodbyes to Mama, I slid into the front seat next to you and waved as you backed the car from the long driveway.

Piled to the roof in the back seat and floor of the car, was a vast assortment of domestic goods. There were bedspreads and blankets of every size and color. Lace and linen tablecloths. Madeira sheets, pillow cases and scarves. Kitchen towels, bath towels, on and on.

During those early days, when you were on the road five times weekly, the car was left piled high with inventory. As the assortment dwindled, you re-stocked from boxes neatly stacked on shelves in a specially built room in our basement. We knew that room was for Daddy's business. Little did we know, however, the sweat and blood connected with his occupation. The strength and determination required to set out each morning, driving up and down the Mohawk Valley to Frankfurt, Ilion, Rome, where customers would vociferate fond greetings as you traveled door-to-door.

This particular morning, I was in seventh heaven as we rode together, hardly a word spoken between us. Words seemed unnecessary. Merely the state of being, father and daughter together, was more than adequate.

Most of your customers were of Italian descent. The warmth and friendship they displayed was obvious, even to my young mind. Mothers painstakingly selected bridal ensembles for their daughters, determinedly filling hope-chests. Nothing was too much for these girls who would soon select mates for marriage.

You were their consultant, providing them with the best that money could buy. They depended on you, week after week, year after year, to help make their homes and those of their children, elegant and charming. As they purchased, you carried them on the books, sometimes for as small an amount as fifty cents per week. Thus, some calls were for collection of mere pennies each week, for items that may have been purchased the preceding month.

There were entire families of customers. In those days, it was not uncommon to have households of three or four generations. Often, you came home with stories about Grandma Destito and the boys. Children were called by first names, but one spoke fondly of the family matriarch as Grandma. Oh, how they loved you, Daddy! What a fuss was made the day you brought your little girl. Never before had I felt so important.

When lunchtime approached, you drove to the main street of Rome and parked in front of a restaurant called *The Home Dairy*. Imagine being taken to a restaurant to eat? I do believe it was my first meal away from our home. It was cafeteria style and I was enchanted as we stood in line, glancing at many varieties, fascinated by aromas. After our selections were made, obviously mindful of kosher dietary laws, we brought our trays to a table, eating as we studied the restaurant's throng of patrons.

What an exciting atmosphere. So, this was the business world. How different from the quiet peaceful environs of our home. This was my father's other world. I felt gratified to think that I had been allowed to share it with him.

Driving home, I was even more quiet than before. There was so much to think about and remember. How many children were fortunate enough to be allowed to spend a working day with their father? As our car headed into the driveway, I knew this day would be entered into my book of forevers.

At The Top Of The Hill

*"The rich and the poor meet together -
The Lord is the maker of them all."*
Proverbs 22:2

Dearest Daddy,

If I were to choose the most important non-material entity aside from love, which you and Mama gave your children, I believe it would be stability. The constancy of our childhood manifest itself in the nine years each of us spent in John F. Hughes School. Older brother Herb graduated from ninth grade, but entered from Roosevelt School as a first grader. Eugene and I both attended from our first day kindergarten through eighth grade, when the alma mater no longer provided an additional year of high school. Austerity of those years looms before my eyes as I vividly recount my entrance to kindergarten and the near decade that followed.

The three-story red brick building stood nearly a city block wide as it overlooked the top of the hill. To enter school on any of three sides, it was necessary to walk up four consecutive flights of stairs, each with approximately fifteen to twenty steps stretching across a vast expanse of the building. In wintertime, an overworked custodian threw sand or ashes on icy steps, eliminating the endless chore of having to shovel stairs each day.

Early each morning, alone, I approached the sidewalk directly in front of the school. In my childish mind, I prayed for strength of body, mind and character to enable me to climb those stairs. During winter days, I often found myself on my knees, climbing with mittened hands to reach the top. Evidently, few children experienced similar misery, for it appeared, I was solely bombarded with snowballs by laughing gangs of juvenile rascals. They seemed to enjoy what I lamented as the torments of winter.

From the first day of kindergarten until graduation and even during many years that followed, I had a recurring nightmare. My dream each night was actually reality by day. Although I succeeded, each time, in climbing to the top of the hill, I continued to dream that I was trying unsuccessfully, to reach my classroom.

Decades later, when our family returned to Utica, our three children attended the school of my childhood. One day, during a quiet mid-afternoon, I deliberately made the trip to school. Was that hill truly as high as I imagined? Were those steps as disastrous? It was actually worse than I had pictured it those many years. This very day, I remain in morbid fear of heights. If we happen to visit a city with lots of hills, I feel ill-at-ease. Even the concert stage leaves me with uneasy feeling, not for the audience, but the fear that I might fall from stage to pit below.

Miss Newberry and Miss Greenich were two middle-aged spinsters who, in softspoken manner, revealed a genial sense of discipline towards their kindergarten children. Although one semester of the school year may have been spent with each, I have a sense of the entire year being melded into simultaneous tutelage. In an exceedingly long narrow room where everything was geared for educational enjoyment, most of what I remember involves having to lie on a cold hardwood floor, small mat beneath my body, for a daily nap. Hazy memories of playing *House* and *Go In and Out The Window* bring to mind a small, frightened child who would rather have remained in the cozy confines of home.

It seemed welcome relief when the year passed and I entered first grade. Miss Hoffman, a genteel lady, predicted that music would become my profession. This seemed remarkably perceptive since her only clues were a vocal rendition of *Robin Redbreast* and piano performance of *The Scarecrow* for the annual spring play. Often, I am puzzled and wonder from whence came my courage, since I recall a fearful youngster engaging in these events.

Second grade held more excitement, but additional terror as I strived to please Miss Glancy. Her hearty laughter and smile were oft exchanged for a display of temper. As a quiet, dutiful child, I felt fairly secure and assured of being in her good graces. Yet, imbued in my memory is the day she took a long rag from the cloak room, bound and gagged the mouth of a classmate whose idle, inquisitive chatter never ceased. Just as I was destined to musicianship, this boy became a renowned attorney. Obviously, his mouthpiece was finally channeled into proper direction.

Our third grade teacher, tall and plump, in addition to many other obstacles, had one serious problem for a woman of her day. Wigs were not the fashion. Her large head with thinning gray hair, displayed prominent bald areas. When her back faced the class as she wrote on the board, one could hear snickers from quickly maturing eight-year-olds. Promptly turning around, she hoped to catch the culprits. The object of young mockery, our sweet spinster was further harrassed by anonymous poetry of uncomplimentary nature.

Several times each week, third graders were ushered into a large, well-equipped classroom. Miss Calmer and Miss McHugo alternated at sounding their pitchpipes as we sang solfeggio. One day, I was asked to play a piano solo for the class. The next time we met, I carried my third grade piano book for confidence, but played from memory, *Spinning Song* of non-Mendelssohn variety. Both teachers and classmates agreed as to my budding musical genius. I, however, was too frightened to think anything!

At the end of first semester third grade, you and Mama were summoned to a parent conference and told I was doing well enough to skip second half. It was decided I would enter fourth grade that January. No one asked my opinion.

First day in fourth grade was disastrous. Mrs. Drummond, our first married teacher, an unusual occurrence at that time, evidently had little patience for students who were allowed to skip a grade. In sudden realization that during the final six months of third grade, one was taught long division, I tearfully raced home at lunchtime, sobbing to Mama that I couldn't divide. With her usual gentle understanding and confidence, Mama sat with me during the lunch hour. When I returned to school that afternoon, I was able to compete with my new classmates at the blackboard. Long division was the least of my problems.

By fifth grade, several new classmates and I had become reasonably good friends. Since our house was centrally located, by walking several blocks north or south, I could socialize with various friends before arriving home. Soon however, I was engaged in afternoon piano lessons twice a week. This would become standard procedure throughout high school.

Miss Spears, our fifth grade teacher, a tall thin spinster with metal-rimmed glasses and hair knotted at the base of her neck, rarely amused her students. Presumably, her serious nature and mine melded into mutual esteem. Sometime during my undergraduate years at Eastman, she and her nonagenarian mother moved to Rochester. We visited several times. Only then did I truly realize she had looked upon me as a favorite student.

Sixth grade imbues my mind with *The Year Of The Mural*. Mrs. Wagner, our austere, long-limbed teacher, was known for her tutelage and annual exhibit of foreign countries. Although we studied English, science, mathematics and all specialized areas, concentrated effort was given each day to the Spring exhibition. By pre-arranged schedule, the entire school was invited to enter our classroom and attend the exhibition. The class was divided into teams. This year, it had been decided that in addition to the usual scrapbooks, topographical maps and essays, we'd create a mural encompassing the entire rear wall of the classroom. Heavy brown paper was stretched across the area and we began. Every country in the world had costumed figures sketched and painted on that mural. The only mural created by any class during Mrs. Wagner's teaching career, it remained in that classroom for many years.

Mrs. Wagner became a favored customer in our store as did many teachers during our school years. I regarded her as an elegant lady. When her back was turned, her handsome coiffure displayed thick iron-gray hair, sides rolled back, with a long, artificial floral arrangement tacked on one side. A different colorful bouquet matched each outfit. Perhaps it was a game she played with her students to ensure that all eyes were upon her each day as she devotedly taught.

Another year quickly passed and I entered the homeroom of Miss Sweeney. The Sweeney sisters, Gladys and Ruth, spent most of their teaching careers at Hughes School, fluctuating between seventh and eighth grade. We were never certain whether our Miss Sweeney was Gladys or Ruth, but each made a memorable impression on her students.

Exchanging rooms and teachers was commonplace during seventh and eighth grade. Teachers interchanged social studies, mathematics and English classes so often, that my mind intertwines the Sweeney sisters with Misses

Gill, Nicholson, LaMore and Casey. Of these, Miss LaMore left the most vivid impression on my mind as well as face. The subject, once again, evades me, though the circumstances remain clear. Test papers were returned and being of very serious nature, I compared notes with a classmate and personal friend. For two different questions, our answers were identical. Yet, beside mine, were two large check marks. Next to hers, nothing. I shyly approached the teacher, asking how this was possible and was given a sharp slap on the cheek. *"Don't ever dispute my corrections again, young lady! When I grade your paper, I know what I am doing."* Well, dear teacher, I surely had my lesson. Never again, did I dispute the word of a teacher. Right or wrong, teacher's word was forever and ever. And ever.

Suddenly, graduation day was imminent. The Wallaces were a prominently delightful and handsome family. Mrs. Wallace, beautiful, blonde and graceful, active in community affairs, had appeared on stage at school when a play was presented during our earlier years. Andrea, our classmate, had two brothers and an older sister. The family resided in a stately mansion on Parkway East. Forbidden territory to the Jewish community at that time. Although classmates were often singled out to attend special events, Andrea invited the entire graduation class to a party at the Wallace mansion.

Once again, Daddy, fear overwhelmed, as you left me at the front door that cold winter night. Wishing to attend so badly, I had no special friend to accompany me. My quiet determination persisted as I waited to enter. Can you imagine my astonishment when a servant appeared at the magnificent oak door and swept me inside? My eyes rotated from side to side, room to room.

Dinner was served by uniformed maids. Black outfits

with white caps and neatly starched ruffled aprons were seen dancing about the crystal chandeliered rooms. Andrea, her lovely mother, father and family, warmly greeted their guests. Suddenly, I was in another world like nothing I had ever experienced and, most likely, would never again witness. It was a strange fairyland.

Soon, I began to picture Mama bending over the ironing board each night as she smoothed the starched wrinkles from my school dresses. I saw her standing before the new white stove in the kitchen, preparing those delicious meals. I imagined the fluorescent light on the kitchen ceiling. The newly decorated large living room in which stood the recently acquired Steinway grand. Our home came clearly to mind as I sat in that mansion. Suddenly, I was anxious to leave, to return to the cozy home and loving parents I shared with my brothers.

Isn't it strange that we can briefly enter another world content to observe? Yet, completely fulfilled as we return to our own environment. Nonetheless, Andrea Wallace will forever remain in my fondest recollections as a classmate who truly made a difference in my life. However, strange as it might seem, she never knew.

Although I remained a high honor student throughout high school, my scholastic endeavors would have remained unnoticed were it not for the recognition of those musical accomplishments. When I received an invitation to perform at graduation, maestro piano teacher consented, by persuasion, to allow my appearance on stage. He scorned public performance by his students, except at his own recitals over which he had absolute control. He doubted our capability to perform at other events. When making rare exceptions, the music performed had to be his choice. He selected a Chopin waltz which I thought rather drab for the occasion. However, it was committed to memory and performed to my potential at that time, evidently well-received by the audience. Moreover, here I sat graduation night, on stage next to Andrea Wallace, Salutatorian and Marcia Dunning, Valedictorian.

At long last, my knee length braids had been cut less than a month earlier, when Mama, encouraged by Aunt Aurelia, curled the remaining short, straight hair with a Toni Home Permanent. I had finally summoned enough courage to ask Mama if I could trade your undershirt for a bra. What a relief when she said, *"Yes, of course, dear."* I sat proudly wearing my new navy blue, silk taffeta dress and maroon leather, ankle strap ballerina shoes. It was January 1949. The following day I would be a freshman at Utica Free Academy.

Shabat

"This is the day which the Lord hath made; we will rejoice and be glad in it."
     Psalms 118.24

Dearest Daddy,

Few memories remain as vivid as those of Shabat, our day of rest. Memories. Sweet, sad. Loving, poignant. Beautiful. The fragrance of Mama's cooking. The kitchen on Leslie Avenue. Our dining room on Brighton Place. Childhood. Teenage years. Countless Shabats with your grandchildren. Even those Friday nights after Mama's death. The mind is a whirlwind of pictorial madness tinged with unbearable remembrance. Exciting to recall, but filled with stinging needles of pain. Each Friday, I am reminded as I stand at the kitchen sink polishing candle sticks.

When Sherri returned from a trip to Crown Heights, the Lubavitch community in Brooklyn, she began lighting Shabat candles in the last of several candelabras used by Mama during her lifetime. When Mama died, you persisted in lighting Shabat candles each Friday night at sundown. We had grown up believing that Shabat candles were lit by a married woman, the mistress and mother of a Jewish home. I realize now, how foolishly impatient I seemed with your continuation of Mama's custom. I felt that the woman of the household claimed this obligation. With Mama's passing, so I reasoned, died also, the weekly ritual of illuminating your home on the Sabbath.

Suddenly, as though with your death, came my sense of maturity and depth of understanding. That first Shabat after your departure, it seemed so natural for me to light candles in Mama's candlesticks as we lit our own. Now, each Shabat finds three sets of candles glowing in their brass and silver elements. The tall, silver-plated candleholders, each with three legs boasting patterns of clustered grapes, bear stately testimony to the fact that they were brought from Europe nearly fourscore years ago, by your mother when she came to this country. The graceful, delicate, brass candlesticks were given to Mama as a shower gift before your marriage. I am surrounded by an aura of love as I kindle both sets. Sherri accompanies me as she lights the third pair of candles housed in the brass set, abbreviated in size, which Mama used during those last few years. The thoughts evoked by the bright Shabat lights are alive, vivid and sweet.

Intensely real, I see before me a little girl, standing with her mother in a brightly decorated kitchen. The shiny white stove has on it several pots from which delightful aromas arise. Mama is standing patiently at the kitchen sink, humming softly as she peels potatoes in preparation for her delectable recipe of scalloped potatoes. Soaking in a pot nearby, are freshly peeled beets. Mama's delicate fingers are already lined with purplish black, in bold evidence of the pains taken to prepare this miserable vegetable. Soon, it will be incorporated into her recipe for mouthwatering Harvard beets.

In a little while, she removes her favorite large wooden chopping bowl from the cupboard. It is reserved strictly for the mincing of raw fish and is kept with the pareve utensils, those used for neither milchig (dairy) nor flaishig (meat). Mama's kosher kitchen is kept with love and pride. We take for granted, and find so natural, the process of separation of meat and dairy products in our kitchen. We have been taught to set the table each night with either meat dishes and meat silverware or the dairy service. It is fun to discipline ourselves in this manner.

Mama has cut up the raw herring delivered that morning by Peshka, the fishman. Soon, it will be chopped so fine it becomes a pate. A bit of vinegar, then some sugar, blending it into a sweet-sour delicacy. She quickly scoops it onto the large yellow platter that matches our dairy set of dishes. Two hard-boiled eggs are finely chopped and sprinkled atop the grey delicacy, the main dish for our dinner tonight.

Mama returns to the stove and begins mixing our favorite dessert, a blend of homemade tapioca. It will be served with whipped cream topping and strawberries. This morning, the milkman delivered two quarts of milk with cream at the top of the bottles. Mama skimmed the cream and it remains in a bowl waiting to be whipped at high speed in the electric mixer an hour before dinner will be served. Next Friday night, she'll probably decide to make a creamy luscious mock-cheese pie with graham cracker crust. She never seems to run out of ideas. There has never been, nor will there ever be, another cook to equal our Mama.

Daddy comes home shortly before dusk, walks quietly into the bathroom and washes before dinner. He always wears an immaculate white shirt with the sleeves rolled up beneath the elbow. He has brought home a large, freshly baked chala, the traditional Sabbath loaf, a braided white bread, specially prepared with egg dough and baked until a rich shade of brown. He pours the wine for himself in the large cup reserved for Friday night Kiddush, the blessing recited over wine on the Sabbath and holidays.

Just as there will never be another cook like Mama, our memories of Daddy's exceptional cantorial chanting remain, never to be forgotten. The Friday night Shabat meal is eaten at the large, beautifully set table in our handsomely cheerful kitchen. Mama serves and sits quietly, watching with a smile on her face as we eagerly devour the delicacies that took her an entire day to make.

Shabat evokes visions of earlier days, before the birth of our younger brother. On Saturday afternoons, we'd climb the darkened stairway to visit Mama's mother, sister and brother. In the dreary kitchen entrance, stood a large black stove. On the bleche, during the entire Shabat, there remained an enormous pot of cholent prepared by Buba. This thick, savory stew was scooped into plates several times during the Sabbath and relieved more observant adherents from further culinary obligation, since no task of any nature must be done from sundown to sundown.

Our visits passed quickly as aunt and uncle fussed over us and sought guises to entertain their only niece and nephew.

During passing years, memories held fast of those Friday nights on Leslie Avenue. Fall. Winter. Spring. Summer. Elementary school. High school. College. Marriage. Our children. Your grandchildren. Sometimes, we returned home with a boyfriend. Girlfriend. Husband. Wife.

Years later, Shabat Friday nights were often shared in our home one-hundred miles away. Another decade passed. Soon, you and Mama joined our family for Shabat dinners on Brighton Place. Fifteen years into our marriage found you both at the Shabat dinner table experiencing, simultaneously, delightful tropical climate. After Mama's death, you continued to share Shabat dinners with us. Now, so different. Yet, painfully sacred as the clock ticked off those final moments.

Time, the evil keeper of our fate, halted those special memories of Shabat. Time, the would-be sentencer of our minds and bodies, initiated us as senior members at our Shabat table. We light candles, cook Mama's delicacies, and chant the Kiddush in tones worthy of your memory. We remain courageous and strong. We hope that fervent prayers will be answered by Hashem no matter how differently from years past, our lives now continue.

For what is life without hope? The memories of yesteryear? The dreams of tomorrow? As the song succinctly states, what is life without . . . tradition?

Harriet & Mac

". . . but thou shalt love thy neighbour as thyself . . ."
Leviticus 19:18

Dearest Daddy,

It was a warm spring day in the early 40's, trees budding, the occasional sight of a robin, when we noticed the large moving van parked on the street in front of their house. The tall, broad stucco edifice did not resemble any other homes on Leslie Avenue. On both sides of the street, from Kenyon Court continuing past the corner of Howe Street to Holland Avenue, the houses were either large, two-story flats or neatly framed bungalows, as single family dwellings were called in those days.

On the same side of the street two houses beyond ours, stood this unusual looking mansion-like structure, its porch fronted by several columns in front of which stood tall evergreen trees. When walking down the street, one had to look closely to see whether anyone was sitting on the porch. The greens and pillars afforded much privacy to their masters.

On this particular day, Shirley, Tweezie and I sauntered sideways, backwards and forwards, bouncing our balls as we tried casually to approach the house. Our curiosity was aroused, but we wished to remain cool, daring not to hope, lest we be disappointed.

He was sweeping the driveway with uncommon gusto. She was polishing the vacant porch floor, evidently brushing each speck of dust created by the moving men as they tracked back and forth, in and out. I left the conversation to my two friends. The words finally came. *"Do you have any children?"* a tiny voice asked. *"No, we don't have children,"* Mac softly replied. *"We are looking forward to meeting the youngsters on this block."*

Shirley and I exchanged smiles as Tweezie continued to babble. Soon, Harriet's soft, but stern voice entered the conversation. *"Yes, we want to get to know you and your friends. But we have some very special rules for you to learn."* Special they were. Indeed. We soon found that visiting with Harriet and Mac was done mostly by invitation.

Another unusual feature of their home was the porch stairway. It was on the side of the house rather than at the front. To approach it, one had to walk for several feet into the driveway. It was difficult to remain casual when we wished to learn whether or not our timing was appropriate. We'd sneak up, half hoping not to be seen, the other part of us praying to be noticed.

"Well, hello there," a friendly voice called. *"How are you today?"* That was the signal. We knew it gave us permission to sit on a step while we talked. It began and ended on those stairs. Somehow, it reminded me of my piano lessons with Maestro. When would I be considered eligible to play the grand rather than the upright? Likewise, when did one gain permission to sit on the porch with Harriet and Mac, rather than on those steps?

Each spring, or at least, every other year, the porch was given its coat of what appeared to be high-gloss beige paint. The pillars were painted cream color. A straw rug, woven in shades of multi-beige, was set on the floor. Several porch rockers and sturdily cushioned chairs graced the area, with perhaps a small table or two on which glasses of lemonade or iced tea were placed for guests. We always imagined you and Mama to be the most immaculate, fussiest pair we knew. Yet, for some reason, one had to place Harriet and Mac at the top of the list.

Now, almost fifty years later, when we dare to compare in terms of today and yesteryear, we realize the uniqueness of a couple like Haarriet and Mac. Condominiums are the order of the day. Depending on which side of the fence we stand, we are confronted by sales personnel with contrasting approaches.

"Of course, we allow children," a smiling face tells us. Glancing at the model, we note a map on which a large colorama gives bold recognition to *The Children's Area*. The other side of the map displays vast expanses clearly marked for adults. At another condo, we are given the evil eye as we approach with our family of three children. *"No children allowed,"* a harsh voice exclaims.

"We merely wish to see the clubhouse," we explain to an adamant guard moving towards us. *"Sorry,"* the retort, his mean, firm exterior pushing us on our way. What has happened to the human race? We wonder.

Harriet and Mac come to mind. We recall the lifetime they spent on Leslie Avenue. I focus slowly and deliberately on each house and the childen raised therein. Next door to our home, the Burgmaiers' four daughters, Chris, Barbara, Rose, Eva. And son, George. A step beyond, lived the Lafferty boys, Billy and Jim. Two houses further, the Plunkett girls, Jean and Sue. Across the road heading up the street were the Prindles, Brian and Bruce. The Galinns, Joel and Barb. Shirley and Joan Dingledein. The Roswigs, Bunny, Mike and baby sister, Jan. Directly across the way lived the Riebers with daughter Barbara, and their huge furry dog, King. Next, were the Lavoie sons, John and Ed. Little Bobby Brooks. Tall majestic Nancy Wildes whose father later became principal of our high-school. In a lofty two-story cream colored house resided the Rubins with daughter Rene, and the Rubbins, unrelated, with son, Ronald. Years later, Mama's friend,

Sylvia, with her husband and son, Jerry dwelled in the tall brown house next door. Just before the very top of the hill lived the Butler brothers, Keith and Brian. From there, one could see the mysterious splendor of Holland Avenue. Another world to the gangs of children on Leslie.

Throughout the years, several homes changed ownership. Youngsters moved away as new ones appeared on the scene. Each time we returned home from college, there was a new name to remember. These names evade me now; but for more than five decades, Harriet and Mac kept track of every single child who lived on Leslie Avenue.

Spring and summer were the best times. Neighbors seemed to be much like birds, hibernating in the winter. Adults were seen only after long snowfalls, when they mustered up enough energy to come out and shovel the snow. Conversations were avoided, with a simple nod of the head to acknowledge another's presence. Children played in small droves, screaming, shouting as they sledded or tossed snowballs into the air, oblivious of anyone standing nearby who might be sweeping light snow from a driveway. No, winter was not a time for neighborly visitations.

But spring and summer. Ah, that first day when one sensed an aroma in the air. That first robin we saw staring from an old gray mound of snow, left behind as grass became more evident. Spring, with its delicate fragrance of flowers preparing to bloom. The sidewalks on which we no longer slipped and slid, but on which we'd soon be rollerskating. There it was, in full view at last. Spring. That invigorating time of year when we renewed the friendships we'd put in cold storage. There again were Harriet and Mac, preparing their elegant porch for company, visits with the children of the neighborhood.

As the air grew warm, Mac was often seen, hose in

hand as he cleaned the driveway. One of the younger children in the neighborhood frequently managed to sneak a look and promptly inform his peers. Within minutes, a half dozen young boys and perhaps a girl or two appeared in their bathing suits, jumping with glee as he hosed them down.

Sometimes, I'd be jealous as I approached the house, sneaked a view and saw Joel actually sitting on a chair! Such nerve. How did he ever manage such a feat? Joel was several years younger than I, with chubby cheeks and curly black hair. He really was cute, I supposed, the type of child considered lovable by the adult world. Of course, Joel was my friend too. We enjoyed riding our bicycles together. Next time we met, I consulted with him and he replied, *"Sure, come on with me. They'll let you up on the porch. Wait and see."*

Presumably, that marked the end of step visits with Harriet and Mac and the beginning of porch visitations. The stairs were lined with white straw carpet on which we were expected to wipe our feet before ascending to the porch.

Harriet and Mac had a mysterious and marvelous manner of talking to children. They knew all the seemingly fit questions to ask and chose appropriate comments and answers to our queries. It was probably their treatment of us as young adults that endeared them.

In the Morath house across the street from Harriet and Mac, resided two brothers, both married. The house, a large flat upstairs and similar one downstairs, accommodated each brother and his wife. Neither couple had children. In the summer, we heard the clinking of horseshoes as the men played in the very long driveway on a special bed of soft dirt created for the game. Clunk, clunk, clunk, went the horseshoes. I could hear them from my bedroom window as I read, leaning on the sill, by illumination of the streetlight in front of our home.

Mrs. Morath, a schoolteacher married to George, had once invited me to their upstairs flat to play the piano. Tea and cookies were served from an elegant silver tray. It was the only time I ever visited with them in the interior of their home.

Children were never invited indoors. As a matter of fact, most neighbors knew one another only by visiting in front of their homes. It was an unspoken practice of the day. Neighbors were hardly ever 'friend-friends'. They were neighbor-friends. Even children rarely entered each others' homes. A knock at the back door was heard. *Can you come out to play?* That was it. No ringing of front doorbells. No entering so much as a back hallway. No sleep-overs. Few, if any parties. Just a simple question followed by a single word, yes or no.

In view of all these things, it was perhaps a small miracle that we spent so much time on the steps and porch of Harriet and Mac who had no children of their own. They knew each of us by name, age, birthday, school, hobbies, awards and achievements. Throughout the years, they added to their records, high schools and colleges, graduation dates, marriages, deaths (yes, unfortunately), our children and, in some cases, grandchildren. They loved us as their own. They showed interest in our lives and shared our dreams. They laughed, sorrowed, listened and advised. Well into their eighties and married for more than six decades, the tales they told concerning lives on Leslie Avenue surpassed greatly, any of today's soaps. Harriet and Mac remain an unforgettable legend.

Alarm Clock A Cappella

"He that spareth his rod hateth his son: but he that loveth him chasteneth him betimes."
　　　Proverbs 13:24

Dearest Daddy,

For years untold, it was an accepted fact that family members analyzed the virtues, faults and personalities of their nieces and nephews. Many of our aunts and uncles considered themselves *mavens,* or authorities on raising the children of their siblings. These studies included lengthy comments on our beauty, handsomeness or lack thereof, and opinions on how we could improve.

The majority of brothers and sisters were lacking in height with several hardly sustaining a five foot maximum. Thus, physical stature became the subject of frequent debate. School class rank, cultural achievements or other virtuous claims did not matter. Analysis concerning height, good looks and for the female segment of our generation, quality of boyfriends, future husbands, lack of romance and fear of the *old-maid syndrome* monopolized family conversation.

Thus, it was that one day during a family get-together, Uncle Herman began to sermonize on the subject of why I had become a pianist and professional musician. *"Of course you spent hours at the piano, night after night. You were a very homely child, had no friends and poured your heart and soul into music. What else could you do? You had no choice. Besides, your mother and father pushed you to practice. Yes indeed, you were a very homely girl."*

Naturally, it was an accepted fact that Herman was the most qualified spokesman amongst the siblings. He had lots of time to study each of his sixteen nieces and nephews, since he and Aunt Edith had no children of their own.

Had Uncle Herman been in our household to witness what actually happened, he could have watched that day, as I approached the piano and began to play be ear, the tune of *America*. I was six years old when you and Mama bought the tall, darksome upright piano for Herb to take lessons. Struggling to make ends meet, you knew that each of your children must have life's finest, including piano lessons. What an exciting day when that piano arrived!

Herb submitted to the plan, but it was I who had the secret yearning of a young musician. You sensed my excitement as I played. Of course, it meant that you soon found yourselves paying for two piano lessons each week, rather than the anticipated one. There was no race for the piano each day. Herb was most obliging and always ready to forfeit his practice time on my behalf.

Several years later, the lofty upright was traded for a more subdued looking 'upright-grand' which made its home in the living room rather than the sun room. Immediately recognizing the difference in tone quality and touch, I was thrilled to have this wonderful new instrument. Within a few years, I shivered with excitement as I entered the living room, incredulous at the sight of a beautiful Steinway parlor-grand!

The more I basked in musical accomplishment, the harder I practiced, hour after hour, day after day. Practicing took precedence over friendships, schoolwork or whatever. It influenced each and every act of my waking hours.

Herb, on the other hand, had different plans for his life. Piano practice was not even at the bottom of his list. It became the subject of daily arguments, Herb refusing to practice and Dad's threatening words, *"You're going to take piano lessons until you get married!"*

One day he thought of an answer. *"I'll set an alarm*

clock for one hour and put it on the piano. When the clock goes off that's it!" In came the large green alarm clock from the kitchen cupboard.

We heard the loud bass octaves of *March of the Dwarfs,* his favorite piece for handling frustration. Bang, bang, bang went the left hand. Five, ten, then fifteen minutes passed. Suddenly, one became aware of thunderous silence. The bathroom door, noticeably closed, could be seen from the kitchen. Soon, again, the bang, bang, bang and return of the dwarfs. Next, the sound of silence and closed bathroom door.

On most days, his timing was excellent. A few moments before the alarm was due to sound, he returned to the piano for a grand finale. Once in awhile, however, he lost the touch for his little game. Then, whoever stood in the kitchen heard the loud, ringing tones of the large, green timepiece sitting on the piano. When alarm clock a cappella sounded, you and Mama knew, as we did, that Herb's practice was finished for another day.

Eyes Down and Watch Your Numbers

"Wealth gotten in haste shall be diminished: but he that gathereth little by little shall increase."
Proverbs 13:11

Dearest Daddy,

It is with mixed emotions that I recall one of Mama's favorite hobbies. Included, were many types of card games. Canasta. Gin-rummy. Bridge. Games popular during a given period of time. There were mah jongg clubs, canasta clubs, bridge clubs. Mama was imbued with the spirit to win. Often, she spent time playing these games with acquaintances whom she otherwise chose not to befriend. When asked why she spent precious time with such characters, Mama quickly replied that it was playing the game that counted.

You preferred to stay home during the evening, reading the local newspaper and a monthly periodical. Mama had other plans. In your amiable fashion, dinner dishes done, out the door you went, into the car with Mama to pick up her sister or a friend, or both. The girls were going to the race track. Fifteen miles from home, Vernon Downs Racetrack was a most inviting place to spend an evening. Several hours later, a bus headed back to town, dropping them at a shopping center around the corner from our home.

Mama adored playing the numbers game, her favorite combination always including numbers three and seven after our street address. Often times, Mama came home excited beyond words. Her eyes illumined as she relished thoughts of the past few hours. Listening as she described each race, one readily imagined the sleek horses hitched to surries, their riders tense and eager as they raced.

Another game that caught Mama's fancy during the early years of your marriage was bingo. Mama hardly ever had company as eager as she, who would escort her to a bingo hall. Her yen for bingo was satisfied during our annual pilgrimage to The Dawn at Sylvan Beach. At the midway, centered nicely between the penny arcade and a redolent hot dog stand, stood a large platform. Within the edifice, long rows of chairs faced continuous rows of tables. Perhaps a hundred or more enthusiastic players sat, while a man with a booming voice began each game with, *"Eyes down and watch your numbers."*

While Mama played bingo for an hour or two, we were allowed to roam the midway with Daddy, returning at short intervals to where she sat. Mama accumulated points during the summer. At the end of each season, our eyes scanned the high shelves where better prizes were displayed. Our home with its polished loveliness, was further enhanced each fall by a new bread box, cannister set, bathroom hamper or scale, won by Mama's expertise at the game of bingo.

With passing years, you and Mama now had three children. The Dawn had become an impractical cottage for our family. Together with other family members, we headed northward on the beach to more suitable accommodations. A few blocks from our new summer haven, Mama discovered another bingo hall. It was not as picturesque and inviting as the midway establishment, but equally satisfying.

In retrospect, I may have been somewheres between twelve and fourteen years old the summer we spotted an unusual looking box perched high on a display shelf at the new bingo hall. *"Daddy, what is that thing?"* we eagerly inquired as we sat with you, waiting for Mama to finish her last game of the night.

"Well, let's see. The sign says it is called a television set. Going to be raffled off at the end of the summer, Labor Day weekend. Looks like some kind of fancy radio with a picture. What'll they think of next?"

Little tickets with numbers were given to every player for each game played. A matching half was thrown into a large bin. Night after night, hundreds of tickets were gathered up and saved for the TV drawing. Bingo players sitting near Mama, carelessly left after a few games, giving no thought to the tickets left behind.

Some folks experience life never mindful of exciting games of chance. Not our Mama. She treasured all tiny possibilities. Surely, something as large and impressive as a brand new television set must not be ignored. She was confident that whatever this new discovery called television had to offer, it would prove interesting and add zest to our lives.

Although Daddy had visions of spending a quiet Labor Day weekend at home, Mama had other plans. Family intact, the car pulled out of our driveway that afternoon and headed for the beach. We must be on time for the drawing. Mama sat at a table arranging her tickets in numerical order. A considerable task involving hundreds of tickets. Soon, the drawing would take place. We laughed as we realized how silly it seemed to contemplate our chances of winning.

But Mama? She carefully arranged tickets and said nothing. Now, the moment had come. The man who called numbers all summer came forward. Stillness pervaded the hall. *"One number and one number only will be called,"* he instructed in a loud voice. *"If nobody here answers to that number a second number will be called. As you all know, the person must be here with ticket in hand in order to be the winner of this here teleevishun set. Ready now.*

Here we go.

"First number we're a-callin' is 970-628-6--3--7. Alright now, anybody here got that number? Ah repeat, 970-628 . . ."

"I've got it! Here! Right here!" Mama's voice was heard with great clarity throughout the bingo hall. The huge TV cabinet with six inch screen and twenty little push buttons was ours.

The fruit of Mama's labors that summer came home that night in the trunk of our car. We carried it into the house and placed it in the sun room. It stood for two years while we waited to receive a television channel in our fair city. Word finally came one day. We turned on the switch to behold Kukla, Fran and Ollie. Such excitement! Mama's love of bingo had truly left its impact on our family.

Erwin's Home Decorators

"Seest thou a man diligent in his business? he shall stand before kings;
He shall not stand before mean men."
Proverbs 22:29

Dearest Daddy,

Sorting through dozens of pictures, I was suddenly captivated by a large black and white photograph of Erwin's Home Decorators. The full size brass bed, just as I remembered, stood slightly beyond the store entrance, adorned by a chintz spread in boldly patterned florals.

My eyes, reflecting deeply into the past, beheld a teenage girl busily arranging shelves behind a glass showcase. How she delighted in sorting exquisite lace scarves, pattern after pattern! Next, she deliberately selected and rearranged some elegant Florentine figurines. Boy with fishing rod. Maiden picking flowers. The lady. Oh, that beautiful head with stately coiffure. Such beauty glazed on china. The figurines were a source of delight to the young girl.

Having completed her latest arrangement, she began redecorating shelves of bath towels. Colors of the rainbow matched with hand towels and wash cloths. Each column must be lined to perfection and color-co-ordinated with its ensemble. When customers entered, she assisted with their selections, unceasingly patient and concerned, fascinated, as it were, by the lavish inventory in her parents' shop.

Each summer while friends searched for work, she knew this exciting job awaited her. Working in her father's store. It never occurred to her that this was also Mama's shop. Mama was part-time saleslady, full time bookkeeper, co-buyer and secretary. Yet, for some nonapparent reason, it was Daddy's store and she was the indispensable summer sales girl who kept it going. When her parents went to New York City on their summer buying trip, they left her the key. This did not fare well with the dedicated help who remained year round. Eventually, the charge became equal, both youth and seniority in amicable command.

Erwin's Home Decorators, then known as Central New York's largest and complete specialty shop, had begun as a small curtain and drapery store in April 1944. With Mama's inspiration, you summoned up courage and opened what promised to be the most beautiful and outstanding domestic shop in the area. The decision to name it after our older brother's middle name, resulted in your becoming known to customers for many miles around, as Mr. and Mrs. Erwin.

When the store opened, it occupied less than half the entire rented area. Behind an elegant interior, was a large stock room and office where you and Mama discussed business, filed back orders, shelved customers' lay-a-ways and made everything happen. Within a short time, business flourished. Erwin's Home Decorators occupied approximately five thousand square feet, with a replete selection of drapery and slipcover fabrics, ready-made draperies, bedroom ensembles, and fine linens. It afforded every conceivable item in fine furnishings for the home, including custom made draperies and slipcovers. Area residents became keenly aware of expert advice received during a visit with Mr. and Mrs. Erwin.

Several years later, you and Mama took another giant step when you decided to buy the building. As a result, you became the landlord of boarders who lived on the second floor. Slowly, we adjusted to the fact that not everyone possessed our life style. The term, alcoholic entered our vocabulary. Yet, we secretly mused about the slovenly characters who occasionally entered the store. They would speak with you for a few moments and quietly leave. They did not cause a disturbance, were well-mannered and kept to themselves. At times, it appeared they were simply paying their rent for the month. There were moments when we wondered. Years later, we surmised that many times they had come to borrow a few dollars. We realized then, the strength you must have possessed to deal with these sad rejects of society. You were strong and firm. Yet, with heart of gold. Just as your family depended on you, Daddy, so did these poor souls.

One day, an undeveloped potential surfaced. You decided to eliminate a superfluous expense by decorating the two walk-in windows surrounding the entrance to the store, rather than continuing service by a window-trimmer. From that moment on, your talent knew no limits. Your flair for arranging spreads, ruffled curtains, drapery materials and a myriad of assorted gift items, was more than obvious. Fellow merchants in the neighborhood often inquired about who was doing your window trimming. They, too, wished to enhance their displays.

One day, as Christmas season approached, we happened upon the scene. You were in the window surrounded by colorful shining ornaments which we knew were forbidden by our tradition. Astonished, I remember asking, *"Daddy, why are you decorating for Christmas if we are Jewish?"* You calmly answered that this was your business. It had nothing to do with traditions practiced at home. As a business man, you were helping others celebrate their traditions. Strangely enough, years later, I found myself offering an identical explanation to our children. They learned as we did, that religion is personal, not necessarily associated with one's life work, so long as that work is honest and morally decent.

The store, as we affectionately referred to it, provided

much of our social life and entertainment. It was meeting place for family and friends. In the early years, Zeda, your father, came to the store, walked back and forth amidst the aisles, hands folded behind his back, and quietly declared, *"Pust . . . Pust."* Yes, there were spells when the store was devoid of customers. Sometimes, for several hours. Daddy's favorite expression for this state of affairs was, *"You could shoot a cannon down Columbia Street."*

Other times, we were amused by the fact that various relatives or friends found the store humming with activity whenever they entered. Unlike Zeda's deduction, these characters thought Erwin's was creating vast amounts of wealth for its owners. Whenever Uncle Herman visited upstate, he made his presence known by dropping in at the store. Mysteriously, fate was invariably on our side. Within moments of his arrival, half a dozen customers were seen browsing in the aisles. Daddy glanced up with an aura of nonchalance. Later in the evening, when the family gathered to visit, Herman spoke to Zeda, extolling the virtues of his youngest brother's business. *"Vuhs hakst du mihr ihn kuhp?"* Zeda replied. Literally, *"Why, are you chopping my head off?"* Implication that Herman knew not of whence he spoke. Again, their father muttered to himself, *"Pust . . . Pust."*

Whenever downtown, we knew we could obtain a ride home by visiting the store at the correct hour. Daddy always had room in the car for extra passengers. During weekends or school holidays, movies at a downtown theater were timed to include the ride home. On Tuesdays and Fridays, after piano lessons at the old YMCA with beloved Maestro, down Washington Street I traipsed, to the store where Daddy, preparing to close, awaited his faithful passenger.

In summertime, I returned to my job, working in the

store. Since Daddy left at crack-of-dawn, I took the bus downtown each morning, waiting at the same corner. The gals at the corner all knew one another. We were the few fortunates who worked in our parents' shops. We proudly acceded to this well-favored custom.

At lunchtime, we walked several blocks to Wildhack's Luncheonette. Joan Wildhack, exactly my age, worked in her parents' restaurant and often served as our waitress. Her pride in her parents' establishment was obvious.

Dollar Day was the most exciting day of the summer. It was held semi-annually. Of course, in January, we'd be in school, but in August we assisted in this wonderful event. Erwin's was well known for its bargain days. On *Dollar Day,* customers were lined up several yards beyond the shop, waiting to rush through the door when nine a.m. arrived. On this unique day, it was a special privilege to act as salesclerk in the store. One felt important as well as intelligent! Imagine knowing prices of infinite items! Sizes of draperies, venetian blinds and curtains! The inventory was immense! One had to be unusually aware during sale times. During later years, after our marriages and advent of increasing numbers of grandchildren, it was an additional treat to select attractive unsold merchandise at the end of the day. Many splendid bedspreads eventually adorned the children's beds as a result of *Dollar Day*.

Erwin's Home Decorators was a thriving business. The result of Mama's and Daddy's blood, sweat and tears. Their indefatigable character. Sometimes, Daddy came home at night, quietly stooped with perspiration as he ascended stairs entering the hallway near the kitchen.

Often, he and Mama arrived home together on days when she worked in the store. Together, they worked and together, they planned for their children's future.

Mr. and Mrs. Erwin were a team. Erwin's Home Decorators was their never-to-be forgotten inspiration. It was a dream realized in days of yesteryear, when every child's wish was to *go downtown with Mama!* Downtown was a place that bustled with excitement. Trolley cars ran the gamut, later followed by elongated shiny buses. Enticing smells pervaded the air from bakeries, candy and nut shops. One sensed the thrilling atmosphere as passersby exchanged greetings. People were handsomely dressed. Going downtown was an important event. Erwin's Home Decorators was indeed a radiant symbol of its time.

Beloved Maestro

"Take fast hold of instruction; let her not go: keep her; for she is thy life."
Proverbs 4:13

Dearest Daddy,

Among treasured photographs is a silver framed picture of someone who greatly influenced the musical nature of my life. Often, gazing intently at his image, I recall that day, long ago, when we first met.

The stairs in the old YMCA building creaked as we ascended. We were surrounded by the brown mustiness of age. High ceilings, wide and rolling bannisters. On the second floor, facing the front window, stood a square table and two large, rickety chairs. Heart pounding, hands trembling, I watched as a door opened a few yards away.

There he stood. If one were to judge by physical appearance, a very thin figure of a man. Sandy haired, fine mustached, freckled and weather-beaten skin. Nothing to particularly overwhelm the viewer. Why then, did I feel this terrible sense of nausea, shivering in fear, an enormous desire to run away and never to return? Why, after four years of piano lessons, were my parents seeking to change teachers? Besides, I rationalized typically as a ten-year-old, all piano teachers were the same.

He exchanged a few words with Mama, asked her to wait outside, and ushered me into the studio. I stood at the entrance, wide-eyed, shaking, and viewed a panorama of photographs. Dozens of them, framed, decorating two long walls. An enormous grand piano, tail facing out, stood at the far end of the room. To my right, I noticed an upright piano against the wall.

He took my volume of Beethoven Sonatas and impatiently hurled it upon a nearby couch. I found the courage to speak, murmuring that I was prepared to play a sonata. He shrugged his shoulders, muttering in unintelligible southern drawl, his doubts as to the credibility of my statement. He informed me in more audible tones, that I might never reach the point of performing a Beethoven Sonata for him. I never did.

He invited me to be seated at the upright piano and play several scales. I quickly obeyed with quivering lips and trembling fingers. He gave me a book of Czerny exercises and a volume of Diabelli Sonatinas to take home.

"If you practice no less than two hours a day, and hopefully, four, following instructions, you'll continue to be my student. Otherwise . . ." And his voice faded. Rumor had it that after half a dozen lessons, many students were asked to leave, never again to enter his studio.

After two or three lessons on the upright piano, I found the courage, one day, to ask how one gained the privilege of playing on the concert grand.

"We'll both know when the time is right," he replied. That was the first time I sensed the slightest bit of mirth in his voice. Yet, I knew my dream of sitting at the grand piano was not scheduled for the near future. Meantime, I became content listening to the deeply resonant chords he produced on the grand in harmony to my shallow sounds at the upright. Simple pieces played by my stubby fingers became harmonious duets as he guided and prodded from across the room.

After several months of steady determination, my lessons became less nervewracking and the shyness less acute. I bolted up those stairs and waited with tremendous anticipation until the studio door opened. Often, I was greeted by a smiling face and a twinkle in the eye. Suddenly, I realized that my lessons were as special to him as they were to me. Music would command my life and we both knew it.

One day, towards the end of the second year, I entered the studio and was told to be seated at the far end of the room, on the bench belonging to the concert grand. Once more, that sudden wave of nausea, trembling lips and fingers overtook my senses and I was struck with a feeling of immobility. Truly, I was not worthy of this great honor. Performing on the concert grand piano of such a magnificent artist and teacher? My entire body rebelled at the thought. A tremendous surge of humility rose within me.

The lesson began. As I played, feeling the enormity of the instrument and swelling of the chords within, I determined never to forsake this unusual privilege. Secretly, I pledged myself to practice a minimum of four hours each day and advance the technique already possessed. At maestro's suggestion, I began taking two lessons each week. Living for these lessons, I had to be reminded of the late hour each evening, when, regretfully, I'd rise from the piano bench in our living room.

Practicing became a great challenge. No assigned piece was too difficult to absorb. Hours were spent puzzling over two or three phrases. My patience was surpassed only by the preëminence of my teacher. His magnitude as a teacher inspired his students to learn. We were his lifeline. His inspiration. He was ours.

Although his immense power at the keyboard belied his appearance, his health was most fragile. One year, he spent several weeks in the hospital after complicated surgery for an ulcerated stomach.

His students were his only family. Each day after school, we visited at the hospital and were instructed to go home and practice! Leaving his bedside, we were overcome with tears. When at last, he returned to teaching, no amount of practice was too great to make up to our wonderful teacher for his illness. In no manner, did we wish to aggravate his condition.

Next to music, DeMolay, the youth movement of Masonry, was his greatest love. Sometimes, he conversed quickly, between lessons, with some of the young men involved in the cause. I did not understand then, exactly what objectives constituted this organization. Nor, did I realize that my teacher was a member of Ziyara Shrine and a founder of the Utica Chapter Order of DeMolay in 1923. I did realize however, that it was a very special part of his life, and drew him several hours each week, from the studio that was his only home.

For eight years, I studied piano with this distinguished teacher. Our maestro knew which of his students aspired to greater heights towards a musical career. Although few words were spoken, we were assured of his interest as he engaged in practical aspects, aside from our scheduled lessons.

For many years, local dignitaries delved into technicalities pursuant to a well endowed music scholarship. Teachers prided themselves on encouraging their young students to win this prestigious award. The younger the better, they thought. Not our maestro. He smiled at the folly of such egotistical nonsense.

"When a student wins that scholarship before senior year, it merely pays the cost of private lessons. Wait until that last year of high school. Then, go after it! You'll receive college tuition. But, just for the fun of it, go ahead and try out in this, your junior year. Good experience. Then, next year, we'll work very hard, you'll compete with a new group of pianists and probably be a winner. A single winner can defend the scholarship for three additional years. And that, my dear girl, will mean four years of

college tuition, if you succeed."

Thus, was I groomed for the wondrous Curran Scholarship. Each year, I returned from Eastman for the spring auditions. Competition was keen, many students lost the award after a first or second time, but determination was my sustenance.

Our maestro was acquainted with Eastman's piano professors. Once again, after my acceptance at Eastman, he assisted in an unusual manner. His awareness of an exceptionally fine piano professor who had served as mentor for several other students during past years, provided further enrichment for my piano study, making me the fortunate recipient of two remarkable teachers. With more than most pianists are provided during a lifetime.

Often, I envisioned myself as the princess in a fairytale. How else could such good fortune be explained? For three years, I was a privileged student of Eastman's Donald Liddell, supreme humanitarian and gifted professor. His strong, but angelic nature, radiated a loving message to his students. It was unthinkable to enter his studio unprepared. During weekly class sessions, when students performed for one another, I daydreamed. Had I really been allowed to pursue piano study with this skillful master?

How does one memorialize the nonpareil teacher in one's life? Must he simply die a lonely, shriveled human being in a nursing home? Forgotten by those whose untold lives he shaped and influenced? Is the half century he spent as a humble, dedicated teacher and performing artist, never to be mentioned again by the inhabitants of a city to which he dedicated his magnificent talent and inspiration?

The silver framed picture of my beloved maestro taken four decades ago, adorns the piano in my studio. It continues to haunt me. I recall his death years ago, and the failure of city officials to memorialize a fine artist wherein he had spent the greatest portion of his life.

Yet, we who reaped the benefits of this humble and dedicated person, are cognizant of the difference he made in our lives. His artistry, humility and devotion. Professor Cecil Davis. Beloved maestro. Symbol of quality.

Girl Scout Cookies

"A man should so live that at the close of every day he can repeat: 'I have not wasted my day.'"
Zohar, Holy Book of Judaism, 13th century

Dearest Daddy,

Nowadays, psychologists thrive on the subject of what makes us tick. Is she, who enjoys the company of large groups, yet, joyously indulges in her own world, considered to have a split personality? I wonder.

Many were the friendships during girlhood. Rollerskating in springtime. Iceskating during long, dull winters. Playing with paper dolls, cuddly dolls, live cats and pups. During teen years, we bicycled to a nearby park, swam at a city pool and played tennis or quiet games of checkers, monopoly and parchisi. Still, I remember the hours spent alone, indulging in activities deemed worthy. Who compelled me? Surely, not you or Mama.

You were both so quiet, hardly ever expressing opinions on what we must accomplish. By an unspoken message, we knew right from wrong and in which direction the worthwhile pastimes prevailed.

As soon as age permitted, I joined Girl Scouts. I remember shopping with Mama for the dull green uniform which I proudly wore with pleasure for several years. A brightly colored scarf was fastened around the neck by a tiny braided guard of official Girl Scout green. With indulgent pride, I wore the dark green beret atop four plaided braids. We were even permitted to wear the head dress of our uniforms during school hours. We happily displayed our scout attire in public. Although meetings were held at night, we wore the uniform all day, showing off in anticipation of the evening.

During the late fall months, Girl Scout cookies were sold. Orders were taken for the cookies, no choice, one kind. Perhaps chocolate chip? The cookies were packaged in large, round, colorful boxes on which Girl Scout emblems were displayed. There was no brochure to enhance our sales pitch.

During the cookie season, we had two to three weeks in which to promote and participate in a contest. The early descent of darkness made me hurry home after school on those days when there was no piano lesson. Then, and always on the weekend, I eagerly dressed in uniform and began door-to-door solicitation. Leslie Avenue sales fulfilled, I proceeded either by way of Howe Street or up the hill and down Holland Avenue. House after house on Emerson and Auburn Avenues. Then, down another block to Van Vorst Street.

"Would you like to buy some Girl Scout cookies?" a plaintive voice inquired, scarcely mustering up the necessary courage.

"Yes, how much are they this year? We'll take two boxes." Rarely, I met with the reply, *"Sorry, we've already bought."*

Written in a little note pad were names, addresses, and number of boxes sold. Then, weeks later, when the cookies arrived, the long route was retraced to deliver the merchandise. Years later, Girl Scout cookies were sold, as to this day, directly, by troops gathered in front of supermarkets or from door-to-door with goods in hand.

I remember selling seventy-five to one-hundred boxes of cookies each year. Always alone, I seemed to thrive on the solitude. Although proud of my sales record, and with a deep sense of achievement, I never recall winning a contest, except, perhaps, within the ranks of our own scout troop.

Each Monday evening at Temple Beth El, we met with our leader, Mrs. Drobner, who lived at the foot of the hill on Holland Avenue. She had a stern, but warm manner, and was loved by the girls. Several of us rang her doorbell midway, on our walk to Temple. Someone was always available with an automobile to drive us the remainder of the way, accompanied by our leader. Afterwards, a small group sauntered to Oneida Street, waited for a bus or strolled further up hill, dropping off friends by the wayside as we walked.

One summer, my girlfriend, Louise, and I became deeply engrossed in domesticity. Either in her kitchen or ours, we usually managed to create a mess while delving into culinary experimentation. The following fall, we proudly sewed our cooking and housekeeping badges on uniform sleeves.

Other scouting activities were surely just as worthwhile. Yet, somehow, in dreams of yesteryear, recalled with deep nostalgic sentiment, are those hours engaged in meandering through streets and avenues bordering Leslie, when I proudly sold Girl Scout cookies.

Sharing Traditions

*"For let all the peoples walk
each one in the name of its god,
But we will walk in the name of
the Lord our God for ever and ever."*
Mica 4:5

Dearest Daddy,

As very young children, there was never a doubt in our minds about who we were. Our heritage remained always before our eyes. In our hearts. It was impossible to forget. Although Shabat, the sabbath to which we looked forward each week, provided a steadfast reminder, simply by virtue of daily deeds, we had cause to remember.

The dietary laws to which we strictly adhered at home, were respectfully heeded at all times. Although puritanical practitioners patronize solely, those restaurants providing strict kosher dietary adherence, we adapted the compromise of merely eating scale fish, fruits or vegetables when dining out. The dietary laws provided a sense of discipline even as we were forever mindful of the richness of our traditions.

Growing up with many school friends of other religious persuasions, it was always understood and graciously acknowledged, that we never ate non-kosher meat or shellfish. Indeed, the difficult occasions were, and still remain, with individuals within our own ranks, who question the need for dietary observance. The adherent fellow is constantly exposed to whims of the callous cad, who has given up his beliefs and wishes you would do likewise.

Although our young, curious minds were roused by celebration of Christian holidays, we did not yearn to adapt the traditions of friends and neighbors. The permissive methods practiced by present day society, tend to magnify their importance. Inquisitive? Yes. Envious? No. We were imbued with the spirit and depth of our own heritage. Sharing traditions was merely done on a superficial level. An attempt to better understand the world about us.

Thus, it was that Shirley and I exchanged inexpensive gifts sometime during the month of December. Contents was unimportant. I delighted at the brightly patterned red and green wrapping, the attractively curled ribbon with little card tucked beneath. Concomitant with the gift, was being allowed to cross the street to her home, into the living room where in the corner, stood an exquisitely decorated tree. My annual pilgrimage! It was not considered a Christmas gift. Nor, was it labeled a Chanukah gift. It was simply a gift because Shirley and her family were celebrating their holiday. It was their way of demonstrating friendship towards our family and I was the happy recipient.

One Saturday afternoon, long after we finished Shabat services and lunch, Shirley came and asked if I might accompany her to confession. This, undoubtedly, was the most powerful request you had thus far received. Especially, from a child of our generation. You were likely engaged in an afternoon nap, for I recall Mama calmly answering that she thought it would be alright if I went, just this once. Hand in hand, Shirley and I accompanied her mother and younger sister to their church.

Entering the cathedral-like edifice, I gazed in solemn wonder at the heavenward ceiling. Intricately carved walls were surrounded by statues of the Virgin Mary and other artistic religious samples. Awed by these surroundings, my mouth probably remained open the entire time. Shirley went into a narrow booth. I could hear her voice. Beyond, in another booth, I heard an occasional male voice. Thus, was my earliest introduction to the religion celebrated by my closest friend. It never occurred to me to invite her to reciprocate by visiting our synagogue. Apparently, I thought that nothing in our world would make much sense to her. We were rather like a secret society. It would have been an invasion of privacy.

Somewheres between our community and another smaller one, a magnificent restaurant was owned by one of your favored customers. Set far back from the highway, Trinkaus Manor was always beautifully decorated with visions of sugar plum fairies, sleighs and evergreen trees. Night lights made it a sight to behold. During December's holiday season, you and Mama set aside one Sunday to dine at this exquisitely charming site. Owing to a cordial relationship with the proprietors, our family received personal consideration and excellent service. Seated by a window, we enjoyed the splendorous view. Ever mindful of your business, we especially noted the newly installed lavish draperies that enhanced the dining room.

It was considered customary to give our teachers holiday gifts. No one was forgotten. Mama carefully chose and wrapped gifts for each. Since most instructors were female, they were bestowed with domestic items from our shop. Pretty little cocktail napkins, guest towels, sometimes a handsomely embroidered handkerchief, were brought home and attractively packaged. Mama chose gifts for our piano maestro at a fine men's shop. Even the weekly cleaning woman received a lavish present from our store. Mama allowed us to help her wrap the gifts and decorate each package with colorful stickers, suggestive of the season.

Cards were received from a few friends of other faiths, who chose holiday time to remember our family. Mama sat down at night and addressed envelopes with greetings of the season tucked inside. We knew these senders mostly by name. Early on, we had visited one of your customers to admire their holiday tree. Now, each year a card was received. Others were former neighbors whose annual greeting helped our families remain in touch. These annual remembrances continued almost half a century.

Sharing traditions has taken on a new meaning. No longer, do we indulge ourselves on the surface. Now, we engage in a fearful mockery of our traditions and those of our neighbors.

Ah, yes *we* must have a tree. Why? Because, if we do not, then our poor, neglected children will be unhappy. They must *not* be different. Everyone will laugh. We *must* be like everyone else. Besides, what does *our* religion offer?

Sharing traditions? Indeed. We've come a long way.

Chanukah, Purim and Passover

"And God looked upon the children of Israel, and God took knowledge of them."
Exodus 2:25

Dearest Daddy,

Sometimes, during early hours of morning, I awakened to Mama's voice speaking on the telephone. *"Hilda,"* I'd hear her say, in the sing-song tone often used when engaged in non-familial conversations. *"Hilda, I'd like a pound of calves' liver. Y - e - s - s. Two pounds of hamburger, but make sure it is ground steak, not any of that other stuff . . . and Hilda, I want two fresh-killed chickens and make sure they haven't been lying around there for too long. Remember now, this is for the Seders. Now, when can he deliver? O.K. . . . alright . . . I'll be home tomorrow morning. Thanks, Hilda . . . have a nice holiday. Yes, Hilda. You too . . . to you and yours. Yes, Hilda . . . you too, dear. Good-bah-ee . . ."*

And during the entire conversation, not a single word of identity. Hilda, the dear soul who worked as number one right-hand gal for the most popular kosher butcher shop in the community, had obviously been born with several afflictions. One evident problem was her eyes, covered by thick, heavy lenses that seemed to go round and round in little circles. Her short, dark brown hair was cut straight in front and back. One might suspect, by a carving knife used in the butcher shop. Her wardrobe consisted of one black dress after another, as though she were forever in a state of mourning. Yet, somewhere in Hilda's brain was a profound ability to recognize the voice of every customer who called. Hilda never made mistakes in either the name or the order placed.

Seders. Holiday. Chickens. Hilda. Could it be? Pesach, our Passover holiday, here so soon? It seemed as though only a short time ago we had celebrated Simchat Torah. And Chanukah, the Festival of Lights, when we delighted in watching the glow of those orange candles, eight nights in a row. Each night, we added a candle to the shiny brass holder on the countertop adjoining the kitchen sink. The idea of receiving gifts never entered our minds. Once in a while, but not on every single Chanukah, we'd happen upon a dreidl or two, the little spinning tops with Hebrew symbols. Then, perhaps a family member treated us to a game of *Dreidl* and a few pennies appeared, much to our delight.

We knew that Chanukah, symbolic of a Jewish victory, was a fun holiday. However, we were also very much aware that Chanukah, as Jewish holy days numbered in the scheme of our young lives, was not on a similar plateau with the holiness of Yom Kippur, Rosh Hashonah or Passover. Nor, did it ever occur to us that Chanukah was the Jewish substitute for our gentile friends' Christmas. We did not need replacements. We were not in competition with the rest of the world. We were Jewish. We were proud and content with our heritage.

A few weeks ago, we had shouted for joy at the mention of Haman's name during the Purim service. With our noisemakers or *groggers* as we called them, we went to schul that night and rejoiced in the telling of Queen Esther's story, repeated year after year in synagogues by Jews throughout the world. During the reading of the Megilla, always in Hebrew, we sat quietly until the name of Haman sounded. Then, we were allowed to use the noisemakers, stomp our feet, even shout with all our might. Until a signal for silence came. *"Alright, alright,"* several men would chant. *"That's enough. Sha! Zol zein sha! Let there be silence!"* We'd sit quietly again, in anticipation, until, once more, we heard the name of Haman. Who knows if any of us knew the story of Queen Esther. I, for one, related to her solely by virtue of the fact that my Hebrew name was Esther. Yet, the holiday of Purim was always welcomed with eagerness and joy in our hearts.

When Mama was actively engaged in Shoshano Chapter, a local Jewish chapter of Order of the Eastern Star, the ladies made beautiful Purim parties for their children. Although not more than six years old, I recall the excitement of being in those lodge rooms with their high ceilings, tall mahogany doors and shiny dark woodwork. The mystery of the interior of that majestic temple of Masonry is difficult to explain, but its simplistic beauty left one so young, with secret enchantment. I clung to Mama's hand, overcome with simultaneous feelings of fear and joy.

Now, it was time to watch quietly, as you and Mama began carrying the huge cartons from the attic to the large kitchen, where they remained on the floor waiting to be unpacked. We were never invited to participate in the monumental task of clearing the cupboard, removing everyday dishes, pots, pans and silverware. Then, washing the Passover dishes, pots, pans, silverware and placing them in those same cupboards. Evidently, you and Mama decided long ago, that it was your task and we were there merely to join in the ensuing festivities.

For the average homemaker, who observes the rituals involved in creating a kosher atmosphere, the Passover festival looms forth each year as a formidable threat. Housewives, young or old, we who observe the bountiful traditions of our ancestors, are well equipped to keep a kosher home. Passed on from grandmother, to mother, to daughter, we know the ins and outs of milchig, flaishig and pareve. Milk, meat and neutral. Growing up in a home endowed with a kosher kitchen, we learned during earliest childhood, that when Mama roasted a brisket for dinner, we drank water at the table and afterwards, a tall glass of hot tea with dessert. Strangers inquiring about various rules of kashrut, the state of being kosher, often try to confuse the issue by asking foolish questions. Why, for instance, do we consider chicken as meat? Chicken is poultry. Why is an egg pareve? An egg comes from a chicken. Why is fish pareve? The dictionary defines fish as an animal living in water.

A bride who opts for a kosher home is showered with untold gifts of pots, pans, dishes, silverware and utensils. She needs at least two separate sets of everything. That is, for everyday use. If family members or friends wish to lavish extras upon the couple, they might further be indulged with expensive china for milk, meat or both. Keeping kosher can appear as an unlimited horizon. Yet, when everything is in place, it is accomplished as easily and peacefully as sipping nectar from a straw. Until Passover. Or, to be exact, two weeks before the arrival of Passover.

Then, even the most amiable, least frenzied homemaker can be found in a state of delirium. Year round? Yes. Why not? It's simple to separate equipment by means of cupboards, doors and drawers. Even a young child encounters no problem when asked to properly set the table for a dairy or meat dinner. But Passover, with its complete changing of dishes, pots and every imaginable item, presents the observer with an almost insurmountable task. However, while housewives busy themselves with countless complexities of the impending holiday, children experience an edge of excitement and pleasure.

Thus, it was with our family. While you and Mama

remained in the kitchen until early morning hours, we'd lie awake in our beds, envisioning the two Passover Seders soon to come.

This year, as in every year past, we would seat ourselves around the large table in the dining room of Mama's sister, in the family's upstairs flat. Their landlord, the butcher who was Hilda's boss, lived downstairs. He and his wife had three youngsters of their own and showed benevolent patience as they listened each night to the cries of our baby cousins. Aunt and Uncle had two little girls and Buba lived with them. Mama's mother, Sarah Freidel, spoke little English and found it difficult to communicate with her grandchildren.

Once, as older brother and I occupied ourselves in a mischievous manner, Buba smoldered inwardly. *"Oh, oh,"* brother exclaimed. *"Buba smells trouble."*

Poor Buba. Into the kitchen she ran, exploding to Mama in her Yiddish tongue. *"Oih, Oih,"* she exclaimed. *"Oif meine sonim gezawgt! Oih!"* Poor Buba. Confused as she was between English and Yiddish, we were accused of saying that our Buba smelled terrible!

Sometimes, with a twinkle in her eye, Buba sat quietly listening to *Uncle Sam* on radio, trying to convince American citizens to *Buy a share of freedom today.*

"Yah, yah, yah," Buba would mimic. *"Buy a Sarah Freidel toh-dayee."* At least this infringement on the English language encouraged Buba to smile.

Waiting for you and Mama to load the car with dishes of goodies, the huge roasting pan, odds and ends, I quietly stood outside in front of the white house with the large porch pillars. Across the street, Shirley and her little sister, Joanie, played with their jump rope. Shirley, a constant playmate, four months my senior, came across to offer me some Easter candy. *"No, I can't. It's our Passover holiday and it began this morning. We can eat only special foods."* She looked at me inquisitively, but with her usual understanding smile. *"O.K.,"* she offered. *"Want to jump rope?" "Not now. Got to go. See ya. 'Bye."*

I climbed eagerly into the family car. I was wearing my new yellow and pastel blue plaid suit. Oh, how I loved that suit! Midst the confusion last week, Mama and I had gone shopping, and I wore my new outfit with adoration. Aside from the beautiful Seders conducted by our father, delicious meals executed by Mama, our aunt, and even Buba, we were treated to a fancy new outfit for each Passover holiday.

Now, family members greeted one another with exuberance and lots of hugs and kissing. Our great aunt, known to us as Tante, and her daughter, Cousin Rivie, were already seated in the dining room. I smiled shyly as Rivie kissed me with a big smile. How could anyone be so kind, sweet and vivacious? *A gem. A doll.* Various family members often referred to her. And in a gentle whisper, as though to conceal the facts from our ears, *But still single*.

When would Rivie's handsome prince come? Each year, she was subjected to the strange custom of having to eat the boiled egg whose shell was burned atop the stove, then placed on the Seder plate. Everyone else ate hard-boiled eggs evenly sliced and covered with cold salt water. We could see the ugliness of Rivie's special egg, cut on the second Seder night, served in the same water, but so conspicuous. *"It's alright. It's alright,"* Mama would intone. *"If Rivie eats 'the egg' her husband will come during this next year. Come on, Rivie, Eat the egg!"*

Thus it went year after year. When Rivie finally married her darling Harry, the following Passover, the burnt egg was given to another victim. I recall eating more than my share of burnt eggs at Passover Seders. A strange custom indeed.

Although our lives were filled with many, many blessings, one of the finest was endowment with a father whose knowledge and chanting skills surpassed those of many Cantors with formal training. Moreover, the formal education you possessed had already been acquired by the age of thirteen, when you came to America. Imagine how much learning took place in those shtetls, the small towns of Europe, to impose such great breadth of knowledge on one so young. Imagine wisdom, education, enlightenment that, properly cultivated, would endure a lifetime. Thus, we listened proudly, year after year, decade upon decade, as our beloved father chanted from the Haggadah, the entire story of the Jews' Exodus from Egypt. You intoned in Hebrew as we followed along, sometimes the Hebrew, at other moments scrutinizing the English, to better understand the text.

At the end of a half hour, midst talking and sipping of wine at appropriate intervals, it was suddenly time to indulge in the meal, so caringly provided by the women in our midst. Each year we were treated to various samplings of gefilte fish. Although the basic recipe for the chopped mixture consisted of blending several types of fish and spices together, shaping into balls and boiling in salted water for two hours, depending on the origin of one's birth, gefilte fish could be either spicy or sweet. Buba's recipe was sweet and bony. Not our favorite. Each year, we'd agree to *just taste a little bit* to the pleading voices of Mama and our aunt.

Following desserts of stewed prunes and Mama's fluffy, light sponge cake, when there was no longer room for another morsel, the wine goblets were returned to the table, as we carefully deciphered codes for remembering which glass belonged to whom. Crying babies, toddlers pulling hemlines, teenagers bullying and, above all, the rich tenor sounds of Daddy's voice as he davened, chanting the remainder of the service. *Time to finish your last glass of wine,* a voice rang into the kitchen. Mama and Aunt Aurelia, both tired but smiling, entered the dining room to sip their final drink of holiness for the evening.

Although one would think the entire evening was enough to last until Passover the next year, such was not the case. The following eve, we bathed and dressed once again, you in your best dark suit, white shirt and tie. Once more, I donned the lovely plaid suit, this time with a different blouse.

Our Orthodox friends and relatives never drove on Sabbath or holy days. However, you and Mama had evidently decided long ago, to eliminate partially, this custom from our lives. We always walked to synagogue on the High Holy Days, Rosh Hashonah and Yom Kippur, but on other holidays we allowed ourselves convenience of using the family automobile. With Mama and brothers each carrying a dish, we climbed into the car and soon greeted our aunts, uncles and cousins for the second Seder.

Years later, we'd remember sharing Seder nights. Some in the home on Leslie, aunt and uncle's home on Parkside, others here and there. But always together. Then suddenly, Mama was gone. We managed to carry on, but it was never the same. Here we were in the sunny south, trying to sustain the tradition and togetherness of former years.

One evening, alone now, you came to our home and conducted the Seder. We were actually managing, at least outwardly, to celebrate in a festive manner. Friends and relatives surrounded the double table area that was set for this beautiful holiday. Esther, an elderly family friend who told us repeatedly, that your davening, your chanting reminded her of her father, had been invited to this Seder. The brightly lit dining room was crowded with our dear ones.

Suddenly, as you chanted the final words of the Haggadah, the narration of the Passover story, I glanced across the room and noted the powerful sadness emanating from your deeply set brown eyes. In a whispering voice you murmured, *"This will be my last Seder."*

Somehow, the meaning of those words were beyond my grasp. I thought, *Daddy is really getting tired. Too tired to conduct our Seders.*

"Oh, Daddy," I chided aloud. *"Come on. You're still terrific. You'll do it again next year."*

Unexpectedly, a few weeks later, the realization of those words crystalized within my mind. The haunting memory of your face as you whispered. *"My last Seder. My last Seder."*

The time had come. The end of an era. We were on our own.

Pastrami On Rye and Apple Strudel

> *"And he hath brought us into this place, and hath given us this land, even a land that floweth with milk and honey."*
> Deuteronomy 26:9

Dearest Daddy,

If the minds of your nine grandchildren were devoid of all memories except one, it would have to be your Sunday visitations. Although there were many periods in our lives when we were living several hours from the homestead, visits from Grandma Mae and Grandpa Moe were frequent. Weekends frequently found you and Mama traveling in one direction or another to see the grandchildren.

Invariably, you arrived laden with packages. Large white boxes tied with heavy string. Bags from which inviting smells evoked feelings of hunger. This ritual did not begin after grandchildren came into your lives. It started as far back as I can possibly remember.

Near the turn of the century, our city's Jewish immigrants, who came from Eastern Europe, settled near downtown. Neighborhoods resembling the shtetls sprang up. Tiny communities of various ethnic groups were common throughout the city. Our Jewish heritage was proudly displayed in the Liberty, Whitesboro and Oriskany Street area.

I am haunted by the vision of a little girl climbing a steep flight of stairs. Or so it seems to her tiny form. She holds her father's hand, long braids hanging down her back. It is Sunday morning and Bessie Black's Deli is bustling with action. Bessie, the only woman behind the counter, is assisted by several men. The customers, not a single lady amongst them, are lined up, waiting their turn.

No one seems to be in a hurry. The men, most of whom wear dark suits and ties, are telling one another jokes and jesting in a good natured manner. Each one wears a wide-brimmed dark, felt hat. The little girl's father seems at ease. He speaks with everyone. Mostly in English, every once in awhile reverting to Yiddish, he visits with each person.

"*Next,*" Bessie cries in a tired voice. "*Hello, Moe, Vuhs machst du? How do you feel?*" He responds in a kindly jovial manner, continuing the conversation in Yiddish. Bessie takes his order, wiping her hands on the long, white apron, now heavily spotted with traces of corned beef, pastrami, salami and tiny reddish-orange stains from the lox or smoked salmon she has been slicing for hours, since crack of dawn this morning.

"*Moe, go sit down at a table,*" Bessie motions. "*A glezele tei. I'll bring you a small glass of tea.*" The little girl follows her father. Together, they pull two curved back, brown chairs to a large round table where several men are engaged in banter. "*Nem! Nem! Take! Take!*" She invites the child, as she sets a dish of apple strudel on the table. Bessie Black arranges with a bakery around the corner to deliver bread, rolls, bagels and pastries to her deli each day. Pumpernickels, caraway ryes, poppy seed rolls, soft rolls, hard rolls, bagels and several kinds of luscious pastries. All are stacked behind the large counters. Simply having to choose can drive a person crazy. Then, what about the types of meat? The lox. Salty or plain? Sliced thick or thin? Sauerkraut? Dill pickles? Reach into the barrel and help yourself. *Nem! Nem! Take! Take!*

Mama rarely cooked on Sunday. Daddy always returned home from the Sunday visitation to Bessie Black, with bag after bag of goodies. We could smell our dinner for several hours before eating. Each week, he made his own special recipe to accompany the delicacies attractively arranged on platters. It was a salad made from all types of fresh vegetables. Dependent on the mood, he began with a base of lettuce and tomatoes, adding carrots, radishes, green peppers, celery. Sometimes, all, occasionally, two or three of these ingredients, were cut up in little pieces and blended with the lettuce and tomatoes. The tomatoes, lush and bright red, were cut in large chunks. In addition to whatever vegetables the salad contained, the distinguishing ingredient was several hard-boiled eggs, sliced and mixed well into the salad. When the large yellow and white bowl was full, a mixture of vinegar, sugar and water, was poured over the dish, and the salad tossed. He proudly displayed his culinary creation and we eagerly ate it with our deli sandwiches, piled high with meat and oozing with mustard.

Although Bessie had a variety of baked goods from which to choose, we always made a second stop at the New York Bakery. The family business begun with the father, was continued by his sons. As one entered the bakery, the aroma made it difficult to exercise self-control. Several counters displayed row upon row of delicately decorated squares, cookies, eclairs, tarts, cupcakes, cakes and pies. In later years, when we became teenagers, Mama no longer baked our birthday cakes. It was easy to place an order and pick it up the next day. It would have been foolish to contest decisions regarding Mama's cakes versus the bakery. Each was completely different and both were delicious.

By the time grandchildren arrived, the bakery was considered the greatest place in the world. Each Sunday, they looked forward to opening the large white boxes containing half-moon cookies, a thick soft dough, decorated with lavish chocolate frosting on one side and vanilla on the other. Never, have we discovered another bakery that makes half-moon cookies as delectable as those from New York Bakery. Although Grandpa's boxes were filled mostly with half-moons, for the sake of variety, a box usually contained sugar cookies. Or chocolate-chip cookies. Or oatmeal cookies. Or molasses cookies. Or apple strudel! And, at all times, a separate box of yummy cupcakes.

Bessie Black soon retired. Almost simultaneously, or so it seemed to our young minds, another deli opened next door to the New York Bakery. Nookie, who received his nickname from neighborhood children who couldn't pronounce his Hebrew name, Noichem, went into business with his wife. They nobly carried on the work of Bessie Black and her associates, as they catered to our community. Many of their customers were Swedish, Italian and Polish immigrants who loved the same delicacies. Although Nookie was open for business on the Sabbath, he adhered strictly to the dietary laws. Separate sets of dishes and silverware were used for meat and milk. If a corned beef sandwich was ordered, it was impossible to be served a glass of milk.

Nookie and his wife went a step further. For the Passover holiday, they completely cleaned and koshered their establishment. Different dishes and utensils were used and a strictly kosher-for-Passover menu was served during the week. Nookie, his wife and daughter always greeted customers with a smile. It was the meeting place with Jewish flavor. Local merchants and traveling salesmen always knew where to congregate for what was laughingly called the Jewish grapevine, news of the day.

A common cliche explains what happened. *All good things must come to an end.* Thus, it was with the deli and bakery of which we were so fond. Sad, sad days they were, when first, Bessie Black, then Nookie's and the bakery closed their doors for the last time. It was a final moment in history. A new era had begun.

Mama's sister, Aunt Aurelia (left) with Daddy's sister, **"AUNT MARIAN"** pictured most likely at Sylvan Beach with Herbert. 1933.

Mama and Daddy on the beach near **"THE DAWN"**. 1937. Our cottage was behind the one pictured.

Daddy with his sisters, Aunt Esther and **"AUNT MARIAN"**. 1982.

In front of **"THE DAWN"**
Herbert and Arlene
with Mama and Daddy. 1939.

Herbert and Arlene, summer of 1940
on the beach near **"THE DAWN"**.

Arlene and Herbert at our home on Madison Avenue, 1938, before we moved to **"LESLIE AVENUE"**.

Our home - 37 **"LESLIE AVENUE"** Circa 1938 - 1974.

Joel, George and Barbara **"LESLIE AVENUE"** 1946.

John F. Hughes School
"AT THE TOP OF THE HILL"

Bridge over Barge Canal, Sylvan Beach where we stayed each summer at
"THE DAWN" - Circa 1940's.

Buba Greenbaum, left, Tante, and Buba Cohen. **"SIMCHAT TORAH JOY AND SORROW"** and **"CHANUKAH, PURIM AND PASSOVER"** 1937.

Buba Greenbaum with Aunt Aurelia and Audrey. 1944.

Mama's brother, Jacob, our Uncle Yunk who served in World War II. 1944.
"THE ATTIC"

CONGREGATION SHAAREI TEFILLAH
(Dedicated in 1924)
Synagogue of our earliest
childhood. **"THE HIGH HOLY DAYS"**
"SUCCCOTH AND SIMCHAT TORAH NIGHT"
"SIMCHAT TORAH JOY AND SORROW"

CONGREGATION HOUSE OF JACOB
AND HEBREW ACADEMY
(Dedicated in 1943)
Where we attended during
our growing up years.
"OUR WEDDING"

TEMPLE BETH EL
(Dedicated in 1930)
"SINGING PRAISES"

"Mac" with various children of the neighborhood, Circa 1956. **"HARRIET AND MAC"**

The year of The Mural - 6th grade - 1947.
Arlene - 2nd row front.
"AT THE TOP OF THE HILL"

Graduation 8th grade - January 1949. John F. Hughes School. Arlene - Front row, left, 1st seat. **"AT THE TOP OF THE HILL"**

Moe Cohen, Daddy as a businessman.
"ERWIN'S HOME DECORATORS"
Circa 1950's.

"ERWIN'S HOME DECORATORS"
308 Columbia Street
Utica, New York
Circa 1943 - 1972

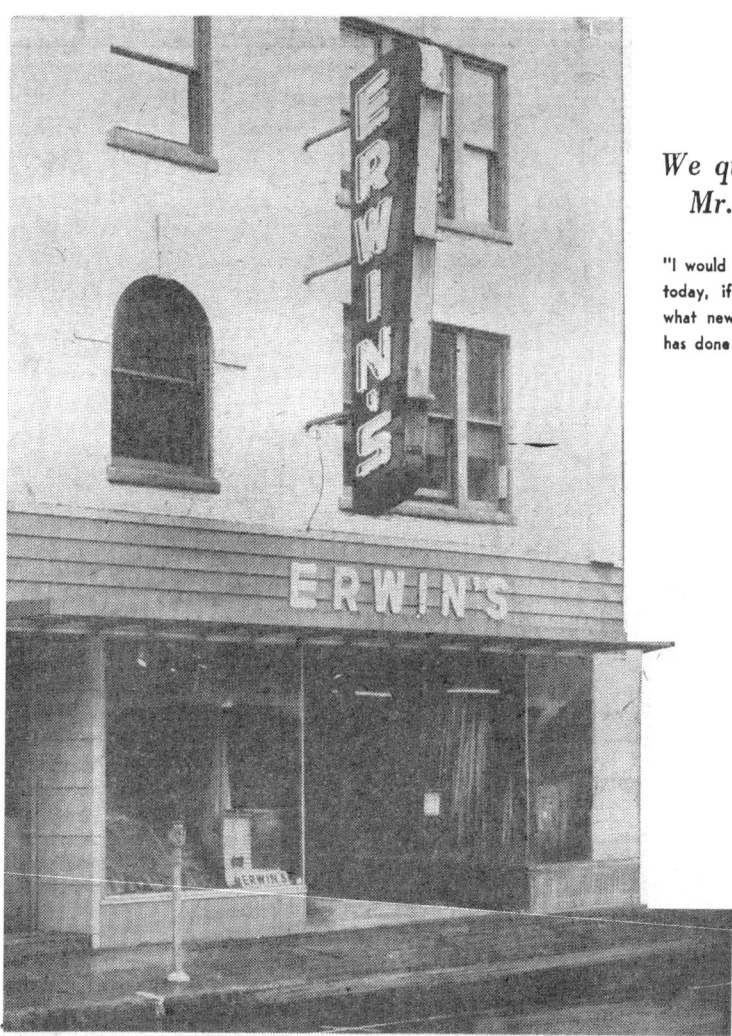

*We quote
Mr. Cohen*

"I would not be in business today, if it were not for what newspaper advertising has done for my business!"

*The families who read these newspapers
are your customers*

THE UTICA NEWSPAPERS

Utica Observer-Dispatch
Afternoon and Sunday

UTICA DAILY PRESS
Weekday Mornings

Professor Cecil Davis
"BELOVED MAESTRO"
February 6, 1950

The old YMCA where Professor Davis lived and taught in his studio.
"BELOVED MAESTRO"

Original music building of
Munson-Williams-Proctor Institute, where our recitals were held.
"CONCERTS AND RECITALS" - Circa 1940's - 1950's.

New Century Club where scholarship auditions were held.
"THE ROAD NOT TAKEN"

Bessie Black's Delicatessen
"PASTRAMI ON RYE AND APPLE STRUDEL"
Circa 1930's - 1940's.

Kleins Retire

New York Bakery and Nookie's Delicatessen.
Nookie and Libby Klein.
"PASTRAMI ON RYE AND APPLE STRUDEL" - Circa 1940's - 1950's.
Nookie's closed December 1976

Mama and Daddy. Summer 1946.
"THE ENGAGEMENT GIFT"

Mama's Mah Jongg Club
"EYES DOWN AND WATCH YOUR NUMBERS"
Circa 1960's.

"SWEET SIXTEEN" - Summer 1951.

1st Row, L. to R.: Beverly Rosenberg, Louise Austin, Eleanor Goldstein, Arlene Cohen, Beverly Bissell, Sandra Schecter, Loretta Bernstein, Judith Stern.
2nd Row, L. to R.: Esther Silverman, Raymond Levy, Rita Klein, Murray Kirshtein, Rita Chrisman, Lillian Silverberg, Dorothy Markson, Elaine Seldin, Jacqueline Goldbas, William Halpern, Marilyn Flack, Michael Slotnick, Toby Schecter.
3rd Row, L. to R.: Larry Savett, Myron Silverman, Myron Nozik, Seymour Goldstone, Daniel Cohen, Jerry Starer, Morty Speiller, Harvey Hershkowitz, Donald Rosenthal, Lawrence Kessler, Arthur Kahn, Stuart Garfinkel, Keith Osber.

High School Graduation Day
June 24, 1953. With Mama and Daddy.
"ALL THE DAYS"

Utica Public Library
303 Genesee Street
A favorite haunt from earliest years. Built in 1904.

Utica Free Academy
"THE SUMMER I LEARNED TO DRIVE"
Original building before annex was built. Circa 1940's - 1950's.

The Eastman Woman's Dormitory
Fall 1953.
"THE ROAD NOT TAKEN"

Eastman Theater adjoining
Eastman School of Music.
Fall 1953.

Election Day

"But thou shalt remember the Lord thy God: for it is he that giveth thee power to get wealth . . ."
    Deuteronomy 8:18

Dearest Daddy,

Often, when opening a drawer of the handsome secretary desk, I find a speech, a letter, a note. Significant words spoken by you or Mama during your respective reigns as head of local organizations. Sitting beside the desk in the large easy chair, I am elated as I study Mama's words.

She speaks of our Pilgrim forefathers. *"It was their idealism, their courage and their sacrifice that gave birth to this land which we all love so dearly. In this mad world of today, it is our heritage to preserve the guarantees of freedom and equality for which they so earnestly strived. This year, more than ever before, must we keep this clearly in mind."*

Mama, how brilliant! How clever! When did you write these speeches? I think back and see you cooking. Cleaning. Washing. Knitting. And I wonder. I think to myself. Was this my mother? How little we surmise as children. Do we ever truly know our parents before they find eternity?

Yet, I remember so well, other ways in which your patriotism manifested itself. Each year, the arrival of Election Day, that first Tuesday in November, was a special day in our lives. Its importance to you and Mama was evident and we knew it was an occasion to be observed with due consideration.

Immigrants who settled in this country the same time as you and Mama, felt strongly concerning their voting privilege. We observed many people of different ethnic backgrounds at the poll. It was obvious to our young minds as we watched and listened. The manner of dress, just a little bit different. A glow in the eyes. A faint smile that tried to conceal the thrill experienced as they voted, perhaps for the very first time. A citizen of these United States. What a blessing!

Since there was no school the next morning, our holiday began the previous evening. We went to bed later, our minds spinning as we reflected on plans for the following day.

"Get up and eat breakfast so we can leave." We suddenly heard Mama's voice coaxing from the kitchen. Soon, we were dressed, teeth brushed and faces shining as we threw on heavy coats and rubbers. It was early November. Yet, the mornings were cold and damp, the fallen leaves soggy and piled high on the sidewalks. Reaching up to the sun room closet shelf, I found the maroon and gray heavy knit hat Mama had made last summer. How I loved that hat! Each long tie of braided yarn had two large, round tassels at the end. A wide collar was attached to the hat. By pulling the ties, an elastic type band held the hat tightly to my head and shoulders. The hat matched a long coat with graceful lines, made of soft wool. I wore the ensemble for several winters. It was probably the only thing I enjoyed about the winter season.

Down Leslie Avenue we hurried, behind Mama. She wore her high-heeled winter boots and black Persian lamb coat. On the front of her coat near the collar, she wore the gold pin that I loved. It was a bird in a gilded cage. The pin remained on that coat forever. We half slid, half stepped, down the long block of Howe Street, crossed the road at Emerson Avenue, and walked one tiny block to Auburn Avenue where we did a left-face. We passed the towering two-story house. Then, the store where we bought our comic books. Another house. And another. Just before we reached the shoemaker shop, Mama stopped.

People were standing on the walk passing out cards. They looked like business cards, but each one had a picture. There were dozens of different cards and we scrambled to collect as many as possible. *Vote for Joe Vincent, your Republican candidate for mayor.* Or, *Your number one councilman, the man who fights for what's right, Bob Norman.* Joyfully delirious, we stooped over to catch the falling cards people dropped as they walked from the poll.

Far back in the driveway, behind the shoemaker shop, we walked with Mama. At the door of the shack, Mama asked us to wait outside. Evidently, voting was a privilege reserved for adults. The windows were too high to see into the little building. Perhaps it was a garage converted for this purpose. At any other time during the year, we'd ride by on our bicycles and peek into the driveway. It was always quiet, apparently deserted, but today there was a humming and buzzing, anticipation of nightfall when the polls would close for another year. Would wise choices be made by the voters? You and Mama discussed nothing else at dinner that evening. Who would be our new mayor? Or, would the same one be re-elected to serve another few years? We listened and tried to match possible winners from the stack of cards collected that morning.

Even more thrilling than our voting with Mama, was what followed. When Mama came out from the shack, continuing down Auburn Avenue, we walked to Genesee Street and the bus stop. We waited a few minutes, then boarded the bus as it pulled to the curb. Riding down Genesee Street was exciting. First, we passed business sections, the post office, Ajab's market, restaurants. Then, suddenly, we noticed the nineteenth century mansions set far back from the street. Stunning red brick edifices, beige stucco buildings and stately homes could be seen block after block, as the bus headed downtown. Several blocks into the business section, we stretched as far as possible and managed to pull the buzzer cord. We descended the high bus steps to the walk, Mama holding our hands. At the corner of Genesee and Bleecker, we headed east, walking past millinary shops and shoe stores. There it was, the same exciting type of restaurant I had once visited with Daddy during our day on the road.

As Mama guided us with our trays, we chose dishes that seemed appropriate. We found a table and removed our heavy outer clothing. Square wooden panels divided the windows facing the street. Passersby glanced at us and continued on their way. Shoppers hurried to and fro. A sense of excitement was all about. The day was gray, the sky overcast. Snowflakes began to fall. Most people were dressed in dark clothing. Yet, in my mind were soft pink, green and yellow pastels, surrounded by a rose-colored aura. Enveloped by Mama's soft smile and mild fragrance, we were at peace with the world.

Singing Praises

"Sing praises to God, sing praises: sing praises unto our king, sing praises."
Psalms 47:7

Dearest Daddy,

It was probably soon after my twelfth birthday, the first time he approached me in the temple lobby. Beth El, our community's only conservative temple, was also used as the Community Center. No one spoke about it. But all teenagers, even those whose parents belonged to a different synagogue, knew that Beth El was the gathering place.

A student lounge, warmly decorated in the style of the day, was open every night except on the Sabbath. *E.A.T.,* the girls' high school sorority, and *A.Z.A.* matched in popularity by *CHI PI PHI,* two fraternities, held weekly meetings in the lounge. Most of us didn't bother to note for what all those letters stood. Nor, were these groups associated with a status symbol. We were proudly assured of the fact that, when we reached a certain level in high school, presented our name to a designated group requesting admission, adhered to the rules of initiation and paid our dues, we became bonafide members. Since there was only one girls' sorority, there was no competition. The boys, however, sustained good-natured rivalry between the two fraternities. We held in esteem, any boy who was a member of either.

Thus, with membership in sorority, Junior Hadassah, Young Judaea, Councilettes and more, I was often at the temple several nights during each week. Membership in these organizations was open to young girls budding into teenage years.

Oh, yes. The lobby of Beth El. I remember his booming voice asking, *"Do you sing? Zoh-prah-no? Ahl-to? Vas?"* His charming Viennese accent, twinkling eyes, and endearing smile fascinated me. Yet, I was frightened by his apparent authority. *"Yah, yah,"* he thundered. *"You kam zu re-har-sol Vensday nacht, ze-ven thirty. Don't be late!!"* And off he strode.

Those words marked my entrance into Beth El's mixed chorus. A relationship that endured for more than twenty-five years. Cantor Paul Niederland had a magical, whimsical charm that ingratiated him with the entire community. He was the musical pillar within Jewish circles and an avid participant in the general musical culture of our city.

Although you and Mama said little about my activities at the temple, I knew that you approved of my association with this fine institution. Parents seldom worried about their teenagers during these times. They always knew where to find us. The temple, a handsome facade rooted in a fashionable block of Genesee Street, could be approached from there or on Scott Street around the corner. Most people used the side entrance, gaining access to the second floor. Yet, this appeared to be the main lobby of the building. The lounge was on this floor, joined by the office, sisterhood gift shop and a large coat room.

To enter the building from Genesee Street, it was necessary to climb a steep flight of stairs, gaining entrance to what was actually the third floor of the building. It housed the large, elegant sanctuary. Long rows of dark brown benches, two long aisles, exquisite stained glass windows, handsome ark and pulpit, all served to make one stand in awe. A last flight of stairs brought one to the fourth floor, housing classrooms for the cheder or Hebrew school.

The Cantor's office that served also as rehearsal room, was on the same floor as the sanctuary. Directly across, was a side door entrance where the choir, preceded by the Cantor and Rabbi, made its entry a few moments before services began. The Cantor's large desk was at the front of the room. A small console piano stood against one wall. At the rear of the study, facing his desk, were two rows of arm-rest desks.

Several older men with resonant voices sat close to the wall. Their laughter and babble could be heard down the corridor. Less than a dozen women busily chatting, noticed as I entered. Another girl whom I recognized from school, invited me to sit beside her.

During those days, when religious ideals were shared by young and old alike, the choir sang every Friday night. Each week on the night of our Sabbath, several hundred congregants gathered in the magnificent sanctuary.

The Cantor was particular, not only about the quality of music and how we sang, but also about our wardrobe. The men wore black robes and skullcaps. The women dressed in white robes. Although the skullcap or yarmulka was not traditional garb for females, we wore white ones to match our robes. During the summer months, before the High Holy Days that come each fall, the robes were sent to be drycleaned. We penciled our name into the collar, thus reserving the same robe for each season.

I realize now, how miraculous were the achievements of our choir. There was not a single member for whom music was a profession. Most of the women were traditional housewives. Perhaps, one or two had training, though not extensive, as an amateur pianist or violinist. Most of the sopranos had strong voices and considered music as their favorite hobby.

The men, both tenors and basses, had effervescent personalities. Each one constantly tried to outdo another in terms of jocularity, wit and vocal activity. Whenever the Cantor gave his signal for rehearsal to begin, it was brought, however, to an immediate and respectful halt.

Since I was one of few who, literally, read music and was studying, the timbre and range of my voice was immaterial to the Cantor. He immediately placed me in the alto section. Choral directors commonly acknowledge the fact, that practicing musicians provide the best harmony, since they read notes correctly and can usually accommodate their vocal range to comply. Years later, the vocal instructor at Eastman insisted on forcing my potential as a soprano. Back and forth I went. Soprano at Eastman. Alto when home for the holy days. Through the years, the alto in me most assuredly won.

Our Cantor, a highly organized and skilled musician, developed an extensive repertoire for the choir and himself as soloist. One of his most amazing accomplishments was the set of brown-covered books we used. Each member was privileged to have his own copy. *"What is so unusual about that?"* one might ask. Unusual indeed. Each book had been precisely handwritten by him. Imagine the time and effort involved to write twenty-five books of music. Each contained over forty pages of notation. Each was specifically written for soprano, alto, tenor or bass. Whenever a new song was added to our repertoire, by some mysterious means, it would be found on a specific page where it had not been the week before. Nor did anyone find a misplaced note. Cantor was definitely a perfectionist.

I am amazed when I think about the quality of music we performed on Friday nights, as well as during the High Holy Day season. Cantorial arrangements by well-known Cantors of the day, were used. They were rich in sonority, emitting lush and harmonious vocal sensations within the great sanctuary where we prayed.

Choir members adapted readily to the fine-line combination of work and play. The high quality of musicianship encouraged by the Cantor, was thoroughly blended with social activities. Merriment was the key note. He knew how to demand the musicianship of which we were capable. He knew how to be serious. One look at the Cantor and we stood at attention. One did not push his luck. Yet, there remained in constant view, that twinkle in the eyes. The warmth of an arm around our shoulder, the pinch of the cheek as he spoke to an individual. The deep resonant voice as it exclaimed, *"Yah, yah. Zoh? Vuhs hert zihch? What's new?"*

When Harry and I married, the Cantor immediately charmed him into the choir's nest. Harry's magnificent tenor voice was indeed a welcome addition. Coming home for the holidays held new meaning in our lives. Being with you and Mama meant most, but singing in the Beth El choir had special significance. Several years and three children later, it became quite a feat to sing at every service during Rosh Hashonah, the New Year and Yom Kippur, Day of Atonement. Back and forth we walked, several times with the children, usually, one or two in a stroller. Then, gradually taller and older, they ambled along behind us.

"Phew, Mom," remarked Howie, our younger son, as we walked in the heat. Hands locked together behind him, he lamented, *"This is a long far."* We continued with the tradition you and Mama observed. Whereas the Orthodox tradition prohibits riding on Sabbath or Holy Days, Conservativism usually allows one to ride to all services. We still walk on the High Holy Days. It serves as a reminder and mild sense of discipline as do many of our traditions.

Our years with Cantor and temple choir continued until his retirement after more than a quarter century. Cantors have come and gone, but none with the spirit, knowledge, musicianship and sense of humor of the man we knew, loved and respected. Camaraderie, that humane quality of good fellowship once experienced among musicians, or simply, people in general, no longer seems to exist. Individuals are enshrouded in their own lives. Apparently, few mind. Most Cantors pronounce themselves immune from obligations inherent in producing a quality chorus. Rarely, does a temple boast of a truly solid, bonafide chorus. Especially, one for which the cantor assumes full responsibility.

Now, many years later, we understand how blessed we were to have within our community, one of the finest cantorial personalities of all time. His voice will long echo in the chambers of Temple Beth El's sanctuary.

Sweet Sixteen

"And they shall put my name upon the children of Israel; and I will bless them."
Numbers 6:27

Dearest Daddy,

Significant among childhood recollections is the grandeur with which you and Mama welcomed each special day in our lives. Birthday. Anniversary. Religious or patriotic festival. Every holiday presented a reason for you and Mama to celebrate. Special dishes cooked to perfection; cakes and other baked goods blended with mouthwatering goodness. Customs observed in detail lent themselves to the occasion.

Birthdays were filled with long days of anticipation as the month slowly approached. Weeks in advance, we wrapped ourselves in daydreams of how the event would take place, type of flowers that would appear on the cake, and what surprising presents we'd receive.

Gifts were practical as well as exciting. An avid reader, often, I received volumes of splendid, classic series or specially bound musical treasures, lifelong pleasure, passed from generation to generation. Big brother and little brother autographed these books, presumably, under parental guidance.

On my sixth birthday, I found a bright blue, flannel wrapped package. Almost the length of a ruler, it was neatly tied with a gray ribbon. Next to it appeared a tiny silver box inscribed with the words, *The Gift Shop*. I opened the little box first and was thrilled to find a delicate gold chain with six-pointed star. Silently fascinated, with awesome delight, I proceeded to don the symbol of our heritage. Moments later, I untied the flannel parcel and was startled to see a shiny, silver, table setting. Two forks, two teaspoons, soup-spoon and knife, all carved in an exquisite regal pattern. A bit confused, I gazed upward and saw you and Mama smiling. Mama sweetly explained that, for the next eleven birthdays, I would receive a similar place setting. Thus, by my seventeenth birthday, I possessed a magnificent set of sterling silver tableware, service for twelve. Enough to enhance any young girl's trousseau. Surely, I was heavenly endowed with parents whose unique foresight embellished, even the social wellbeing of their children. Whose parental servitude enabled their children to reap the benefits of a physical, psychological, educational and spiritual world, with meager financial backing. Hard work and imagination were the two basic ingredients used to achieve wonders.

As years stole quickly by, I became momentarily disenchanted by simple family gatherings to celebrate birthdays. I secretly yearned to invite teenage friends. Sensing my discontent, Mama often promised, *"Don't worry, dear. When you celebrate your sixteenth birthday we'll have a wonderful Sweet Sixteen party. We'll rent a hotel room and you can invite lots of friends."*

A few weeks before my sixteenth birthday, I timidly began reminding Mama about her promise. We rented a beautiful room at one of the grand hotels downtown and proceeded to make plans. Naturally, there must be a 'date' for each girlfriend invited. No matter that three or four gals sat beneath the flowered walls, while one of the more popular feminine creatures was romanced by half-a-dozen males. In our silly minds, there was that tete-a-tete combination symbolic of teenage years. Decades later, we laughed to see our own teenagers congregate in groups. Even on the rock-n-roll dance floor, with little regard for whether or not one had a partner.

The hotel room was decorated with lavish amounts of twisted crepe paper in bright colors. Large clusters of balloons hung high in the air. A juke box had been rented for the evening. By push of a button, we selected dozens of top hits; the more popular guests displaying latest dancing techniques. Thirty-three happy teenagers, well-dressed in various styles of the day. Each one carefully versed in proper etiquette, came bearing gifts for their honored hostess. Thirty-four teens, with age variance less than two years. Well-mannered boys wearing suit or sport jacket, tie, polished shoes, shining faces, spoke much rehearsed pearls of wisdom to the girls with whom they danced.

From Nookie's ever popular kosher deli came large, tempting platters of delicatessen. Salads enhanced the long buffet table at one end of the room. Delighted by enticing aromas filling the air, guests began to overcome their shyness and indulge in refreshments. Centered on the table, was an overly large, round cake decorated with treble clef, staff and large cherries for notes. The bakery had outdone itself. Music was obviously the theme for happy events in my life.

There was no differentiation of class within the community. We were united by our common heritage. Within our midst, stood young men and women, the children of area merchants, accountants, doctors. Some affluent. Others struggling to provide their families with niceties of life unknown to them, when they lived as children in *the old country*. We were completely unaware of who waxed rich, who was poor. We welcomed the presence of one another in public school. Then, stood together in prayer at the synagogue. Whether for Bar Mitzvahs, Confirmations, or Sweet Sixteen parties, we were as one.

I gaze with nostalgia at the large photograph taken during my *Sweet Sixteen* party. What has happened to her?

To him, whose face smiles back at me? Many years later, contact remains with less than a dozen. Most have married. A few are divorced. At least two have passed on to eternity. Do they have children? What are their families doing, especially, to continue our heritage? I wonder as I gaze, keenly aware of what has befallen our children's generation. I recall with silent sadness, our daughter's attempt to host a party. Fifteen written invitations requesting RSVP, totally ignored, and appearance of three guests when the moment arrived.

Our daughter studies the photograph in disbelief. "Mom, really, was that truly your *Sweet Sixteen* party? The girls dressed in such gorgeous outfits and all the boys in suits! And Mom, you mean to say they were all *Jewish* and wanted to *date* each other? I can't believe it! The guys acutally danced with you? Wow! And they ate *kosher* food and thought it was great? Come on, Mom. You must be putting me on."

Careful now. Don't say it. "When I was a young girl . . ." Hopefully, we've come full cycle. That my granddaughter will tell the happy tale of her *Sweet Sixteen* party. They say that every other generation repeats itself. *Halevei* . . . May it only happen.

The Summer I Learned To Drive

*"Hear counsel, and receive instruction,
That thou mayest be wise in thy latter end."*
Proverbs 19:20

Dearest Daddy,

While very young children, we learned in what esteem you held the family automobile. Used far more for business than pleasure, you attended to its every need, making sure it was in mint condition, as you traveled throughout the valley, engaged in business.

After the store opened, leaving Mama in charge of the sales help, you departed for several hours each afternoon, to continue the pattern of catering to home clientele.

The car was kept polished with proper oil changes, full gas tank and frequently, new tires. We were taught that ownership of an automobile meant responsibility. It was a prized possession.

The summer of my seventeenth birthday, my friend, Jerome, volunteered to teach me to drive, provided that my father allowed us to use the family car. Although Jerome had no vehicle of his own, he did have a driver's license. Daddy, it may have been blind love, or confidence in me as well as my friend, that allowed you to consent to this project. Whatever the reason, I accepted in sheer gratitude and amazement. Jerome and I were on our way.

At the far end of a woodland area, overlooking the city, was a lookout point at which stood a large statue of an eagle. This area, truly a lover's lane, was commonly referred to as *The Eagle*. It was forbidden territory for nice girls. Each weeknight that hot summer, as we supposedly took off for destinations unknown, Jerome encouraged me to drive along these wooded paths and practice ascending the hills. Most convincing in his rhetoric, he persuaded me that the driving test would eventually be a series of ascending and descending hills. Naturally, I obeyed this masterful professor and propelled our shiny blue and white 1952 Plymouth to the infamous statue.

Upon arrival each evening, Jerome instructed me in parallel parking the vehicle to obtain the best view. Motor turned off, we quietly glanced towards cars on either side and watched activities in which our neighbors were engaged. I presume Jerome sensed it would be of no avail to display amorous intentions, having, as it were, an uncooperative partner. As it grew dark, Jerome verified my skill in turning on headlights, guiding the Plymouth around shrubbed areas, and carefully descending the steep hill.

Ironically, for one whose fear of hills lasted during more than a decade of childhood, I surely learned to master them behind the wheel of an automobile. That fall, shortly after entering my senior year at Utica Free Academy, I took several lessons from a driving school. I don't think Jerome and I had much occasion to put the car in reverse. After half a dozen lessons that specialized in shifting in reverse, I felt ready to brave the test. On that memorable day, since Jerome, my mentor, had returned to an out-of-town boys' academy, the school driving instructor brought me to the driving test bureau.

Behind the wheel for several moments, I turned down a busy, narrow street. Suddenly, a siren screamed from behind. The test administrator grabbed the wheel, steering to the side of the road. Surely, I thought, that was the end. I would fail my first road test.

"I'm sorry," he quickly apologized. *"I would never wait during an emergency, to learn whether you knew what to do."*

My license arrived two days later. I was now a full-fledged driver. Mama and I took our first trip downtown the next day. Mama was very proud. She was relieved to have another driver in the family. We cheerfully drove down Oneida Street, headed for the square that merged with Genesee. Our eyes became glued to a police officer dressed in blue jacket, with shiny brass buttons and visor cap. His arms spread lengthwise as he blew his whistle. Traffic slowed down to a crawl. Since Mama and I planned to visit a specific store before closing time, I decided to carefully proceed around traffic and continue on our way.

The police officer was extremely rude as he jumped aside our car, so close he could bang on the window. I decided to open the window and ask what was the matter.

"Young lady," he gnarled. *"Don't you know what it means when a policeman spreads his arms in front of you and blows his whistle?"* Well, Daddy dear, at that very moment, I became conscious of grateful realization that my father was one person who had confidence and believed in his daughter.

Once, upon returning home, you observed that the left wall of the garage was suddenly too close to the left fender of the car. You never said a word. You simply hired a carpenter to come and alleviate the problem. It appeared, the more I drove, the more we encountered these little problems, but always things that could easily be corrected. Mr. Burgmaier, our swarthy, kindly nextdoor neighbor, often came and lifted the rear left fender off that dreadful wall. How it got there, I never quite understood. That summer, my seventeenth year, I finally learned what it meant to be trusted, loved and handed the keys to the family automobile.

The Road Not Taken

*"When wisdom entereth into thine heart and knowledge is pleasant unto thy soul:
Discretion shall preserve thee, understanding shall keep thee . . ."*
Proverbs, 2:10,11

Dearest Daddy,

Only in retrospect, are we allowed to feel and think the thoughts of unfulfilled possibilities during our lifetime. How different would life have become had we taken an alternative path? Poets have written about it. Authors have penned fragments of imagination concerning the innumerable what-ifs in life.

Mine, finds me a teenage high school senior, preparing for a musical career. Exciting days, filled with hour after hour of preparation for auditions. Scholarships to be won. Recitals to be played.

This year would be my only opportunity to win the Curran Scholarship that provided college tuition. As a winner of the piano competition, I would be entitled to compete three additional years to retain the scholarship.

The weeks before auditions were fraught with anxiety. Students, portraying a sense of indifference, congregated in the music room before band and orchestra rehearsals, casually discussing the pieces they planned to perform. Trying to conceal their innermost desires to be a winner, while they wished one another good luck.

Finally, the day of days arrived. Auditions were held in the New Century Club, downtown, in the heart of our fair city. A large, rather cold room housed an old, but well-preserved concert grand piano. At a long table, sat three stern looking, bespectacled judges, writing pads before them, as they studied individual applications. During the morning, they had heard dozens of students perform on woodwind and brass instruments. All that remained, were the piano and voice auditions. We congregated at the back of the room, awaiting that flick of an eye and low-toned voice that would call someone's name.

Who would be first? Was it best to get it over with? Or would it be wiser to be the final performer? If I played first, would they remember the good points as they sat through one after another of these budding young pianists? Questions and answers plagued my mind. Suddenly, I heard my name called by one of the judges.

Walking towards the front of the room, I set the music before the judge who had called my name. I would begin with a Bach Prelude and Fugue, continue with a Mozart Sonata and end with Chopin's Fantaisie-Impromptu. At any moment during one of the pieces, we had been forewarned that a judge might interrupt and ask that we proceed with the next number, or continue with another section of the same piece. We were trained not to interpret the meaning of these interruptions. Heaven help us if we began to feel that we had played so poorly, or made so many errors, that we were no longer in competition. Concentration was the key word.

A few months earlier, I applied, and had been accepted at Ithaca College. During a weekend at the campus, I auditioned for the chairman of the piano department. How thrilled you and Mama were when I received a congratulatory letter of admission, as well as a scholarship award. It was an unexpected prize! There was no doubt as to the school I planned to attend.

That day in the Century Club, at the end of auditions, one of the judges beckoned me to come forward. *"Where do you plan to attend college next fall?"* he calmly asked, as I stood in awe. Imagine, this famous personality speaking directly to me! *"Well, sir, I've been accepted at Ithaca College. I've also been granted a scholarship as a piano* major. I'm planning to attend Ithaca College School of Music."

"Now, young lady, before you make any decisions, why not apply at Eastman School of Music?"

"Oh, no sir, I would never be accepted at Eastman. That's for really talented students. No, I'm pretty sure I'm going to Ithaca."

He puffed several times on a thick cigar, the twinkle in his eye showing obvious amusement. *"Now here, take this address and send to Eastman for an application. Do it right away. Don't delay."*

Hesitating, I took the paper from his hand. *"Why not?"* I told myself. *"What is there to lose?"*

We sat up late that night, waiting for the newspaper to appear on the stands. With nervous fingers, I scanned each page. There it was, headlined. *Curran Auditions Held.* My name . . . it was there . . . *first prize for piano to . . . daughter of . . .*

Within a short time, the letter arrived from Eastman scheduling an audition. Soon, I would be on the first of many train rides, arriving at Eastman dorm for the weekend. No audition ever made me as nervous as the one on that eventful day. I entered the dark hallway and found the door with the number I had written on a slip of paper. My heart raced as I knocked. There was no reply. Slowly, I turned the knob. Pushing the door inward, I saw the smiling face of a bespectacled man. He was calmly puffing on a thick cigar. Suddenly, it made sense. Here was my judge from the Curran auditions.

As years went by, I often pondered as to the turn of events in my life. What-if I had not auditioned for the scholarship? What-if this judge had not adjudicated and encouraged me to apply at Eastman? What-if I had never moved to the city where soulmate hubby and I met? What-if? What-if?

Union Station

"For in much wisdom is much grief: and he that increaseth knowledge increaseth sorrow."
Ecclesiastes 1:18

Dearest Daddy,

Rarely, does one find an opportunity to successfully relive the past. Most often, we choose wisely, to never look back, always going forward.

Yet, several months ago, your grandson, Howard, invited his mother to accompany him on a trip, of all places, back to her alma mater. He planned to take a jazz workshop and suggested that I take a piano workshop during the same week. The idea was so inviting!

Soon, plans were under way, airline tickets purchased, and dormitory reservations made. With the final tuition payment, came sudden, frightening thoughts. Why had I done this foolish thing? The expense was exorbitant; the thought of staying in my old college dorm was ridiculous! To compete in a piano workshop with young, future concert pianists, working towards master and doctorate degrees? Putting my frustration in the back of my mind, I began preparations for the trip. Soon, the day arrived and we drove to the airport, said our farewells, and boarded the plane.

Several hours later, we were met at the airport by an old girl friend. We spent hours visiting, reminiscing and even, yes, reliving the past. This was obviously going to be fun! Later, in the dorm that evening, I noticed two friendly faces across the hall. Nor, did they appear any younger than I. *Guess I'm not the only old fool to walk these halls,* I mused. The two gals spoke and soon, we were engaged in conversation, laughter and giggles in every sentence. They admitted having seen me earlier, strolling down the hall with a tall, handsome young man. They wondered how I had managed to trap an admirer so soon. And one so young! *"Your son!"* they howled. We began to attract the attention of other friendly associates, who, apparently, held the mother-son team in high esteem. Evidently, it was an uncommon occurrence at the school. Mother, a professional musician returns to alma mater after twenty-eight years, accompanied by musician son.

The week flew by. Classes continued hour after hour. Between sessions, we were expected to hole up in a practice room and practice the daylights out of ourselves! What a fantastic feeling. Freedom to practice without interruption by thoughts of what to serve for supper, cleaning the kitchen, answering the telephone or finishing the laundry. It was wonderful to escape to the world of unreality. At the end of the week, we participated in concerts. Howard's jazz ensemble appeared on stage Saturday evening. I was so proud! Then suddenly, sad, as I realized I was the only family member there to listen. Two evenings before, I felt a glowing sense of achievement as I sat at the concert grand piano on stage and actually performed. A miracle, I thought to myself.

Early Sunday morning, we boarded a bus and headed for the city of my birth. As we traveled along the highway, my mind calmly and favorably reminisced. Suddenly, I realized, we were there. We stepped down from the bus and then it hit like a boulder, clumping to the bottom of a hill.

We were standing in front of Union Station. Noticing my hesitant expression, the busdriver suggested, *"If you need a telephone or want to call a taxi, go into the station. They'll help."* I wanted to run as far as possible. Yet, I was drawn to enter. I gazed sadly around the empty shell. The huge, marble pillars stood as always, polished gleaming white. Heavy dark brown benches, dozens of them, row after row, unoccupied, were surrounded by vacant newsstands and coffee shops on either side. At the end closest to the street, remained a small ticket office used by train and bus officials. A deep sea of nothingness. I retreated quickly from the world about me. And then . . . I saw you.

It was a gloomy winter day. The train had brought me home for the long weekend and Thanksgiving holiday. My face was radiant as we met. Your slight figure, always properly dressed in a dark suit, tie and overcoat, topped by a wide-brimmed felt hat, hurried towards me. No picture will ever be clearer than the one before me now. We exchanged hugs and kisses as we jumped back over the tracks, into the station and out the front door, where the car waited.

The station was bustling with activity. There was never a place to sit, if one had a few moments to spare, waiting for a train. A pleading glance sometimes succeeded in convincing an individual to move, pick up a bag or two, and make room for another to sit down. The coffee shop with its high marble stools, remained open twenty-four hours round the clock, enabling travelers to wait in comfort and enjoy a snack. The large newstand carried newspapers of big cities. The *New York Times* was always available. Magazines of every color and description decorated the wall beyond. Five cent candy bars and chewing gum of every brand could be chosen for one's trip. Morning, noon or night, a ticket agent was always on hand.

In the days when you and Mama were courting, Union Station even had a hall where dances were held. Union Station was *the* meeting place. We loved the endless bedtime stories. Even city buses going towards downtown, displayed signs reading *Union Station*. The tracks where a little girl walked behind her father to synagogue, were the same tracks whose trains brought her home from college for so many holidays. The tremendous appeal of train stations during early days of the twentieth century, lingering into the fifties of college days, is simply impossible to convey to one who did not experience it. No picture can help to communicate the thrill of visiting Union Station during those times. Very few college students used other means of transportation. Even classmates from the midwest or deep south, took the train, but only at the beginning and end of the school year. Sometimes, we brought a classmate home for those short, mid-year holiday breaks. Many students lived too far to travel. It didn't occur to many, to travel by airplane.

For my eleventh birthday, you and Mama decided to grant me an excursion to New York. That summer, I accompanied you on your semi-annual buying trip. No journey was ever more exciting! The train thundered and roared into Grand Central Station! My eyes beheld a sight that overwhelmed my young mind. My youthful heart was unbelievably thrilled by the hotels, skyscrapers and restaurants of New York. Yet, it was the train that endeared me forever.

Once again, your form danced before my eyes. I looked all about, but there was nothing. A voice called in the distance. *"Come on, Mom. It's time to go. The car's here."* I felt a hand on my shoulder. Howard . . . your grandson.

The Engagement Gift

*"Her children rise up, and call her blessed;
Her husband also, and he praiseth her."*
Proverbs 31:28

Dearest Daddy,

What was the quality, the magic which you and Mama possessed, that enabled you to teach your children two significant aspects of life? Was it the time in which we lived? You both knew the arduous strife and difficulties of mere existence. This enhanced your appreciation of natural beauty, as well as the material possessions you gradually acquired. These were the two lessons bestowed upon us as we grew from childhood to adulthood.

We were encouraged to relish in the beauty of nature, to explore with young friends, venturing on long bicycle rides and hikes in woodlands near our home. The innocence of life in those years allowed for space between parent and child. We did not know the fear of consequence so restrictive in today's society. Children could be free as butterflies.

Yet, in our home, we were also taught to appreciate the beauty of material desires. The parlor was a special room with distinctive trinkets, collected by you and Mama during the early years of your marriage.

The handsome secretary, with its well chosen volumes, held my interest all during childhood. It stands now in our living room, just as you and Mama enjoyed it during more than fifty years of marriage. I am still fascinated by those books, a classic library in which I love to browse. Sitting in that soft, plushy lounge chair of half century, with the gracefully polished, small, round library table adjacent, it is easy to read and dream, to study or reminisce, to be alone with one's thoughts. Yes, material items are important. They help to inspire, yet, we must constantly be aware lest they initiate feelings of frustration, greed and trauma within our minds.

The bureau in the bedroom which you and Mama shared, was adorned by an elegant dresser set. Sometimes, when Mama asked me to dust, I was inwardly thrilled, for it meant that I could touch and examine each piece, slowly, yet with no malace of forethought. This special collection had been your engagement gift to Mama. It remained questionable throughout the years, whether it meant more to her or to you.

The obvious, yet, unspoken romance behind it, continued to remain mysterious. The set contained a beautifully shaped mirror, brush and comb; a three-piece manicure set, lady's shoe horn, two tiny, round, covered containers (for which I saw no practical use), two larger, covered receptacles (one with a specially carved hole in its cover, in which I mischievously stuck my finger whenever dusting); a hexagon shaped tray with lace under glass; a nail buffer, clothes brush and elegant, miniature mantel clock. The entire set appeared to be made of mother-of-pearl. It had tiny daisies with touches of dark green leaves decorating each piece.

I knew why you had lovingly chosen it for Mama. It was, most assuredly, something to be used, valued and held in high esteem by a lady, a woman of the times. Mama was surely that lady.

Her nails were always beautifully manicured, her coiffure painstakingly done in the fashion of the moment. I sat in awe, as she buffed her nails with that delicate mother-of-pearl instrument, so perfectly suited to her ladylike manner.

Being a lady came naturally to Mama. I still hear her

voice saying, *"Now, act like a lady."* Or, *"Be a lady. That is not how a lady laughs."* Sometimes she would say, *"But dear, that is s-o-o-o-h unladylike."*

I study the dresser set, your engagement gift to Mama, as it now adorns our bedroom vanity. It reminds me of the love you and Mama shared. Of those moments behind closed doors, so sacred in marriage; yet, apt to be taken for granted by children. Only when those years have dwindled into eternity, can we truly sense their meaning. Yes, Mama was a woman who knew true love and you were the husband she cherished.

One day, during that final week, as I entered the room where you lay, you cried out in anguish. The tears would not subside, as you begged me to mend the broken comb. The pathos in your voice was evident, as you despaired that the set had been an engagement gift to Mama. The broken comb matched so well, the broken heart of a man whose wife had pre-deceased him from earthly existence.

In the spiritual world, where we no longer relate to material aspects of life, I fancy you and Mama sustaining the romantic pathway traveled here on earth. Oh, that your spirits would soar to boundless heights and meet their wondrous destiny.

All The Days

"And remember that the companionship of Time is but of short duration. It flies more quickly than the shades of evening. We are like a child that grasps in his hand a sunbeam. He opens his hand soon again, but, to his amazement, finds it empty and the brightness gone.
        Yedaya Penini, 14th century

Dearest Daddy,

Whenever I become inspired to elevate my thoughts, I like to ponder. To contemplate the meaning of simple words. For instance, one might dwell on the word *time*. A comprehensive dictionary defines *time* by stating, *all the days there have been or ever will be; the past, present and future*. My favorite antiquated volume of words, with worn cover boasting a half century of use, rests nearby on the desk. Let's see what it offers about the meaning of time. *That in which events are distinguished with reference to before and after, beginning and end; the measurable aspect of duration.*

I do so fancy the first. Yes, quite so . . . *all the days there have been or ever will be*. I am lured by the eloquence in that poetic interpretation. Time can be our friend, but all the more, our enemy. Is it not strange that we are unaware of how it is wasted? Until, suddenly, glancing over a shoulder, we realize it has left us behind? Few of us have the power to predict the future, suggesting how our time should be spent. Only by glancing backward at the passage of time, evaluating both the good and bad that has befallen us, can we even begin to analyze our lives.

When the *time* in our lives is taking place, we have only the past with which to compare. And the hopes and dreams of tomorrow. When we've lost optimism and hope, for better things to come, usually, we realize that the time is rapidly approaching when we shall depart from our earthly existence.

What would it be like if that huge apparatus pictured in science fiction movies, were suddenly to become part of our lives? Today, I have chosen to be whirled back to the nineteen-fifties scene, at the corner of Hopper and Genesee Streets. The sky is blue on this breezy June day. Although the high school graduation class had nearly two-hundred girls, each proud, young maiden managed to select a white dress of delicate distinction.

Mama helped me choose a soft and simple costume, its sleeveless, button-down front capped at the shoulders with a slender fluted edge. The girl graduates carried a large bouquet of yellow daisies. With spike-heeled white shoes, I felt like a sophisticated model. Enter *time* to play an unforgivable trick. The thick, dark brown hair, loathed during those teenage years, now appears lush and lovely in the photographs. What must I have been thinking? Suddenly, I penitently recall the arguments with Mama. *"Honestly, dear, your hair looks beautiful. Trust me. Your hair is gorgeous; the perm turned out great."*

On and on, it went for endless hours, day after day. *"No, I'm a freak. I KNOW I'm a freak! My hair looks disgusting! It's too thick. It's too dark. I wish it were blonde. Even purple would look better than this."*

On *Coronation Banquet Night,* I was given the dubious honor of performing as graduation class piano soloist. There I sat, alone as I recall, in some hotel. At Maestro's insistence, we performed from memory. I remained in a corner, petrified that I would surely make a mess of the performance. Several hundred students mulled around, while dozens of teachers scurried to kick off the affair. Occasionally, a classmate approached and offered to sign my yearbook.

I glance at the book now. So many, many years later. Has time been kind? Did any of our foolish notions come to be? I am amazed by the number of autographed notes that refer to my pianistic qualities in complimentary manner. *Keep up the piano work . . . you're great . . . honestly . . . Sandy . . . Good luck to you. You certainly know how to play the piano wonderfully . . . Carolyn . . .* Here's a true optimist speaking . . . *Best of luck to you always. I'm sure you'll have a brilliant career in music . . . Helen . . .* Time has really dealt a blow with that one. *You played as wonderfully tonight as usual. I see sure success in store for you . . . Dodo . . . I know I'll see you in Carnegie Hall some day . . . Rita . . .* Well, Rita, not unless we both travel to New York to attend the same concert.

Bob had similar aspirations for me. *Best of luck in the future and send me a ticket for your first concert in the hall.* Sabra spiced her note with humor. *Lots of luck to the gal with 'da fingers' . . . I know you'll go far in music!!* I suppose she was correct concerning one aspect. We have, after all, re-located our home from north to south, a goodly distance!

Harvey's comment was cute and sweet. *Although you sell curtains, it will never hide your talent.* Several classmates, including Harvey, had parents who owned shops on the same street as our store. Coming and going to work, we often peeked at one another as we sauntered up and down the block. If we were nursing a *crush,* we peeped through a window as often as we liked, pretending to window-shop as we went to business.

Norman, another musical admirer, a buddy in the high school orchestra, autographed, *Good luck to a swell piano player. I enjoyed your recital.* Once again, time reminds me. Did I actually play an entire graduation recital from memory? Performing music of the masters? A phenomenal achievement. How did I manage it?

I never recollect being admonished by you or Mama

on the adversities of *killing* or wasting time. In retrospect, I am convinced that I was a child worka-holic. There were never enough hours in one day for me to fulfill the plans about which I dreamed. It was generally assumed that students of our ethnic background excelled in their studies, as well as music. It never occurred to me to become an exception. *Of course,* I graduated as a high honor student. *Certainly,* I chose to further my education. *Surely,* I was considered a more than adequate pianist. There was no doubt in my mind that time would take care of the rest.

Now, I experience the strange sensation of time racing from our lives. I have the frenzied feeling mentioned often by you and Mama. Touched and influenced by the ebb of time, we try, desperately, to control its flow.

We were young and foolish, sure-footed and optimistic as we bid our farewells. Teachers autographed our books with happy little quips . . . *To the girl with the raven tresses* . . . On a front page of the book, in large, bold handwriting, I note the words of Miss Milne, our counselor.

Although visits with Miss Milne were brief, they seemed to have substance. With few words from her, we were encouraged to go forth once more. To try just a little bit harder. Now, as I linger within these pages, her words confront me. I dream about *all the days there have been or ever will be; the past, present and future.* And I read. *May you find true happiness, Arlene . . . Ruth Milne.*

Mama's Showers

*"She perceiveth that her merchandise is good;
Her lamp goeth not out by night."*
Proverbs 31:18

Dearest Daddy,

It is easy to look back now and realize how beautiful our lives were for so many years. Time after time, our family was blessed with happy events, good health and good fortune. How is one to know that such is not the lot of everyone? Indeed, we look about, complacent with our lives, noting a friend's illness, a neighbor's financial distress, the death of an acquaintance in the community. Temporary *food for thought*. A kind word or two, as we pause to acknowledge another's misfortune. Then, on our way once more, as we continue with the riches of personal daily existence.

Suddenly, we awaken one day to the staggering silence. I remember the little game you and I played after Mama's death. You were determined to continue living in the apartment. The pain rose to boundless heights, whenever we entered and saw the beautiful furnishings and knick-knacks accumulated during your marriage. Whenever we visited, I attempted to conceal my feelings. Deep inside, the hurt would remain forever. Each day, when I called, you answered with the usual goodnatured lilt in your voice. *"Yes . . . and what is it now?"*

"Daddy, why don't you say hello? How can you always be so sure that I am at the other end?"

"Who else would call? Only my daughter. The telephone never rings. It is very quiet here."

Though you were my dearest Dad, nevertheless, I had the remainder of a busy life apart from you. Family life at home, indeed, flowed at a hectic pace. The only stillness I knew, lurked within your apartment, like a veil over darkness.

Peace and quiet for which we pray, during hectic years of childrearing, sneak up totally unannounced. Stillness screams at us and all around, can be seen photographs illuminating happiness. And, of course, Mama's notes and lists:

SHOWER GIFT LIST: Sunday, March 29, 1959
Mrs. S. Kowalsky, two crystal
Mrs. R. Myers, one crystal
Mrs. A. Galinsky, one and one-third crystal
Mrs. H. Antovil, one dessert plate

Mama's bridal showers, like each task she performed, were an absolute work of art. Mama worked harder and remained more organized, than anyone we ever knew. Her accomplishments in any area, whether cooking, baking, sewing, crocheting, knitting, public-speaking, bookkeeping or making showers, were assumed to perfection.

What was the meaning of this list? How does one give a gift of one and one-third pieces of crystal? It was all very simple. That is, when organized by a hostess like Mama. The bride selected her china, crystal, and silver patterns at a designated shop. Guests were asked to visit the shop, then decide, according to personal taste, how much to spend. Thus, what part of the crystal, china or silver, one wished to bestow upon the bride. Consequently, one could receive four pieces as a single gift from three guests. So ingenious, Mama's list reading, *Mrs. J. Block, one and one-third crystal.*

Moreover, at the conclusion of the shower, if more than the usual dozen glasses were received in any one of the designated five sizes comprising a complete set, Mama paid a visit to the shop owner. She exchanged and created a perfect sixty-piece set of crystal glassware. Likewise, went the arrangement with dinner set, and for some brides, silverware.

Mama's showers, in partnership with an aunt or two, were given for several nieces, as well as her own daughter and daughters-in-law. A few weeks before each event, Mama worked in the kitchen late at night, the table covered with an array of floral patterned handkerchiefs, colorful ribbons, straws and common pins. Mama had discovered how to make a miniature umbrella to place beside each setting as a take-home favor for every guest.

Each shower was attended by well over one-hundred guests. Thus, year after year, before every shower, Mama created these beautiful little umbrellas galore. Each umbrella was tied at the top with a tiny satin ribbon. So lovely to recall. Yet, in retrospect, it was probably one of manifold acts and deeds in which Mama's genius, inspiration and talent were taken for granted. We expected Mama to create, show remarkable artistry, and be the height of perfection. We were never disappointed.

The bridal showers were held in one of the local elegant restaurants of the day. Occasionally, guests were entertained in a graceful chamber adjacent to the ballroom of a hotel. Sometimes, the bride-to-be received friends in a country club setting. Of one thing we could be certain. Mama's choice of locale was always harmonious with the taste she exhibited in every other phase of planning her events.

Although luncheon was served, Mama made the decisions on choice of menu, from appetizer to dessert. Carefully observing dietary traditions, the main dish was usually a fruit plate or broiled fish. The bill of fare was embellished with her own baked goods, candy and nuts. Oohs and aahs of approval were often heard by delighted guests.

Repeatedly, it has been said that youth is wasted on the young. So be it with bridal showers. Did we ever take time to wrap our arms around Mama in sheer love and gratitude for the wondrous things she achieved in her unassuming manner? Her domesticity wrought miracles upon us. But youth, sweet youth . . . never knew. Now, on age-yellowed paper, the shower guest lists confront me. If only . . .

Our Wedding

> "My beloved spoke, and said unto me:
> 'Rise up, my love, my fair one, and come away.'"
> The Song of Songs 2:10

Dearest Daddy,

Have you ever reflected upon the word, *letter,* and its true meaning? A letter can say a great deal. Or, so little. Letters may have hidden meanings. They can heal or rend the recipient. The dictionary defines letter as *a written or printed communication of a direct or personal nature.*

Some families barely express any form of communication during an entire lifetime. Others find verbal expression impossible, but solace in the form of notes and cards. Letters might be written to members dwelling within a single household. Such was the nature of our dear Mama, who was able to express deep wisdom and love in letters to her children.

On February 5, 1959, we received one of Mama's precious letters. Did I say precious? Herein, note another unique quality of letter-writing. Assumably, a letter acquires importance simply by virtue of creation. Not true. Rarely, is a letter meaningful to its recipient upon first reading. It must be read and re-read. Days, months, ah, yes . . . years later. Thereby, is found the ultimate secret. The recipient must develop sensibility equal to that of the correspondent. Foolish is the mortal who discards letters as they arrive from friends and loved ones. One must, in fact, be a saver when it comes to letters.

Long ago, on that February day, Mama's letter arrived from Miami Beach, simply stated, *"I just wanted to drop you both a line to tell you how happy I am for you."*

Indeed, who would have thought, during foolish,

naive girlhood, that a mother could be happy for her daughter? Only now, so many years later, comes understanding of the depth of love in that sentence. Both possible and true, was Mama's happiness for her daughter. Her love and sincerity were unceasing.

Less than three months earlier, Harry and I had met. Handsome and polite, he stole my heart at first meeting. Mama, too, proclaimed love at first sight. Whenever Harry and Mama met, her face illuminated with a delicate smile, as she greeted him with an ingratiating, *"Hi, Harry."* Thus it remained until the very last moment. Harry always caused Mama to smile. There existed a special affinity between them.

When we met, Harry was an automobile salesman, deep in the throes of a national contest. Fourteen salesmen throughout the states, would be awarded a trip for two, to Mexico. Several weeks later, he was in first place for his dealership, standing a good chance of becoming a national winner.

We never discussed marriage, only the contest. Mama quietly asked what would happen if Harry won. Would he propose marriage? Were we likely to marry quickly? It was mid-winter. Relatives could not be expected to travel north during the cold, miserable winter months. What were our plans? We had no plans. We had just met. A girl did not discuss marriage with a new beau, merely because he was in a sales contest.

Daddy, you and Mama usually took separate trips to Florida, so that one could remain in the store. You had recently returned, and Mama looked forward to leaving. Her final question was whether she should take the trip. What-if Harry won the contest and we decided to marry?

Mama was encouraged to depart. After being in Florida no more than a few days, she wrote that special letter.

Moreover, her disappointment at having a month's vacation end abruptly, never entered her mind or that letter:

"We were just thrilled to hear that you won the contest, even though it means planning everything in a hurry. However, all that is unimportant. The most important thing is your happiness and I don't need to tell you, I'm, sure, that Dad and I wish for you both, a long and happy life together, with all, and if possible, more, of the blessings that we ourselves have enjoyed."

Harry and I were married on February 19th, in a beautiful Orthodox synagogue. Since time was of the essence, tumultuous plans were made, even invitations printed overnight and received hardly more than a week in advance. The wedding gown was tailor created in four days, hemline shortened one night before the ceremony. Since the choicest kosher caterer in the area was not booked for that Thursday evening in mid-winter, we acquired his services. Beautiful flowers adorned pulpit and chupuh, the marriage canopy. Centerpieces graced the tables. You and Mama brought two passengers, our beloved Rabbi Ginsburg, whose synagogue we attended during childhood, and dear Cantor Niederland. It was a perfect wedding, attended by eighty guests.

Thanks to wintry blasts of the season, our fondest desires were readily available and anxiously met. Unlike those of the ever popular June bride.

In my mind, I continue to portray our wedding night as a beautiful, warm evening in June. Only much later, did we realize that February 19th became known as *The blizard of '59*.

Mama's Driving Lessons

"Oh that I might have my request; and that God would grant me the thing that I long for!"
Job 6:8

Dearest Daddy,

Both sad and glad are the little notations discovered, that were made by you and Mama throughout the years. The variety of thoughts is endless. Some hastily scribbled. Others, as was Mama's style, neatly typed on stationery. Somehow, it leaves one feeling melancholy to witness the innerselves of parents so dear. Their feelings. Their hopes. Their dreams. And now, no longer.

One day, not long ago, discovering a small stack of notes, odds and ends, I was stunned to read a neatly typed notation that began:

> "*Start car: 1. Hand brake on.   2. Clutch in.*
> *3. Turn key . . . little gas."*

The instructions continued:

> *"Car starts on first, when going 15 - 20 mph lift foot up from gas (click) and car goes into second. Car starts in second, lift foot up from gas and car goes into third (click). When at stop light or sign use foot brake instead of hand brake to stop car. Hand brake only when stopping car permanently."*

Thus, was the typewritten page filled with instructions on how to drive.

My heart instantly ached with thoughts of Mama trying desperately to learn how to drive. Such a perfectionist. Perhaps, the world's singular person who thought to type personal instructions for driving an automobile. Project one step at a time, and in writing? Never! Into the car, experienced driver aside and zoom! Gas pedal first, worry later. Not Mama. Each and every thing in life was done with precision, inch by inch, step by step.

Although you were an extremely accommodating husband and father, we recalled from earliest childhood days, Mama's frustration at being unable to drive. A constant acknowledgement of defeat. A hindrance in her life. Inability to achieve something which, to most individuals, was a simple accomplishment.

Mama calmly acquiesced to acceptance of rides from friends and, mostly, to the good-natured chauffering provided by her loving husband. Friends were unhesitatingly offered transportation to or from meetings, always, with assurance of overwhelming generosity, as you made stop after stop along the way.

Suddenly, one day, we heard sounds of discontent.

"I'm going to learn to drive if it's the last thing I do!"

Soon, a car appeared, Mama climbed into the driver's seat and slowly headed down the street. A series of driving lessons. Presently, conversational hints concerning pending driving test. Then, nothing.

When Uncle Milton became a family member, he volunteered to teach Mama how to drive. Each day, he appeared and, eased by his winning smile and good nature, Mama went driving.

Years passed. We were married, living several hours away. One day, Mama called, her excitement evident.

"I'm really sure this time. I just know I'll pass the test. I'll take it tomorrow."

I spoke encouragingly. *"Good luck, Mama. I know you can do it."*

Next evening, she called, her tearful voice evident. *"I failed the test,"* she cried.

"Mama," I implored. *"Take it again. This week!*

Don't quit now! You'll pass the second time. Please, Mama, take it again.''

Mama never took another test. Never again, did she mention driving. There was always a sadness about her when requesting a ride. It remained throughout her life. That deep sense of failure. Forever.

Tears fall as I read the final instruction on the neatly typed sheet of stationery:

''When you want to increase speed quickly, use foot shift.''

Chicken Soup and Tsihmes

"Many daughters have done valiantly,
But thou excellest them all."
Proverbs 31:29

Dearest Daddy,

    Incredible though it may seem, Mama's extraordinary talent and cooking expertise did not rub off on me. Assuredly, when setting my mind to it, I cook what most family and friends consider, a more than adequate meal. Tasty, even artistic in style. Yet, I'll stoically manage to use dozens of little short-cuts that never would have entered Mama's mind.

    Why peel those nasty little potatoes and risk slicing a finger? One may, just as readily, open a few cans, place them in a baking dish, add a dash of pepper, tomato sauce, and heat in the oven. Sweet potatoes or yams, thus prepared, respond to a similar technique. I can, just as easily, cheat my way through a delicious potato kugel, but when it comes to lokshen kugel, noodle pudding, I conscientiously concoct it from beginning to end.

    One is challenged to find various ingredients with which to combine the standard noodles, shortening and eggs. Toppings vary. Sometimes, crushed cornflake crumbs, wheat germ, or whatever cereal pleases the fancy at the moment. Actually, whatever stands conveniently on the kitchen counter. The mixture itself, when made as a dairy dish, contains cheese and sour cream. My interpretation fluctuates from cottage or farmer cheese to cream cheese, and, unlike Mama, whatever brand sour cream is on sale.

    Mama used only top quality ingredients at all times. To me, quality varies with price. I love a bargain, whether in food, household or clothing items. I pride myself on the fact that our two sons, when the time comes, will be more than appreciative of their wives' cooking. Never, will they ridicule a meal placed before them, by boasting of their mother's culinary skill.

With true confession, I unabashedly admit that it has been years since a poor, blameless little chicken was gently lowered into an immense pot full of boiling water. Instead, shortly before the dinner hour, spooned into a smaller pot, is the proper measurement of powdered ingredients contained in a round, plastic canister. The label reads, *Instant Soup Mix . . . Tastes Like Homemade Chicken Soup!*

Usually, during the Passover holiday season, I splurge, and make Mama's matzoh ball recipe. When followed to the letter, her recipe creates the most delicious kneidlach, as they are called. Upon noting the family's zest as they partake, I promise myself that I shall make kneidlach at least every other month. Soon, however, I find myself cleaning the refrigerator once again, for the fast approaching holiday of Passover.

With admiring love, I recall the manner in which Mama prepared chicken soup. For reasons unknown, Friday night Sabbath meal never consisted of traditional soup, chicken, and trimmings. Yet, on an occasional Sunday and all holidays, we were assured of a mouthwatering dinner, consisting of the soup and roast chicken. For the meal preceding the Day of Atonement, we were served boiled chicken, directly from the pot of soup. Boiled chicken, rather than roasted, left one without a lingering sense of thirst. Less indulgence in spicy food made it easier to fast, especially since the fast consisted of refraining from *all* food and drink for more than twenty-four hours.

Usually, the chicken was boiled in soup to assure

proper seasoning. Mama sometimes made chicken salad afterwards, an additional delicacy to enjoy during the week. Naturally, the soup was cooked to perfection. An onion, skinned and whole, a tomato, scalded and peeled, then added to the pot, a bit of salt, a dash of pepper, and above all, made with the delicate hands of one who loved to cook. Years later, trying to imitate Mama's style, I created soup that was either too watery, too spicy, too salty, even at times, too bony. Yes, imagine cooking the soup until, with a sense of remorse, I realized the chicken had disintegrated into bits and pieces of bone. I now appreciate the connotation associated with the joke of treating a sick person to chicken soup. It is not the soup itself, but the love encompassing it, that makes the difference.

Mama's tsihmes surely executed a sight and taste never equaled. First, potatoes were peeled and divided into two sections, those to be grated and blended into a potato kugel or kneidl, a rather large dumpling; and those that were diced into the tsihmes. The latter, a mixture of carrots and potatoes, was cooked with a bit of flour and sugar, blended to Mama's perfection. Into a large roasting pan went the precooked mixture. Next to it, Mama carefully set the kneidl. In a frying pan, she seared an impressive looking koshered chunk of lamb that was sliced later that day, after it became succulent while roasting in the oven. Everything came together in a delectably wondrous manner. Although several of Mama's dishes became favorites with her children and other family members, it is possible that her tsihmes was rated number one on the list.

Small wonder that she became daring enough when we were very young, to make this special recipe on Thanksgiving Day. Naive and trusting souls as we were, Mama convinced us that tsihmes was turkey. It was no more than a sign of the times. Since you and Mama both agreed, assuming, indeed, that our lives were very sheltered, it was many years later that we finally knew the difference. Somehow, it did not matter. If given a choice today, I'd gratefully and enthusiastically opt for Mama's tsihmes.

The Brihs

"Now therefore fear ye not; I will sustain you, and your little ones."
            Genesis 50:21

Dearest Daddy,

"What is a brihs?" I remember asking you and Mama. Never, did the answer seem adequate. Always, an evasive reply. During those years, children were not worldly and wise. Neither, did parents give direct answers. Always, secret, hushed happenings behind closed doors. Only years later, after becoming the mother of two sons, did I realize the significance of this religious ceremony.

What a fuss you and Mama made for the brihs of each grandson. Imagine the joy of celebrating this simcha seven times! For months ahead, Mama baked, to assure that the freezer would be stocked with dozens of cookies, in the event that the next grandchild was a boy.

Brihses were held in Albany, Rochester and Utica, but distance never mattered. You were always there. Mama prepared many other delicacies to compliment the delicious dainty sweets.

Invariably, no matter where the brihs was held, you assumed responsibility for personally escorting Cantor and his lovely wife to the event. Cantor was a mohel, trained to perform circumcision according to tradition, while Fanny, his dear partner, served as able assistant. Each baby was special, lovingly cuddled before and after the ceremony, as she held wine-saturated cotton to the tiny mouth. Love was the key word associated with each ceremony.

Cantor and Fanny officiated at the brihs of five grandsons. Mix together two heaping cups of affection. Stir with unmeasured amount of tenderness. Add a dash of spice, a bit of sweetness. Blend with meticulous performance of ceremony. Ultimate result? A memorable brihs conducted by the Niederlands, with Daddy at the helm and Mama's delectable delicacies. Indeed, a significant event to cherish.

Louise and Butter-Puff

"Even in laughter the heart is sorrowful; and the end of mirth is heaviness."
Proverbs 14:13

Dearest Daddy,

One day, in the fall of the year, Louise and Butter-Puff fortuitously entered our lives. Louis, your first-born grandson, a third grader at that time, spoke of nothing else upon his return from school. From that day forward, we lived, breathed, and conversed in terms of gerbils.

"Gerbils?" I suspiciously questioned. *"Are you sure? Better learn the correct name. I've never heard of such an animal."*

But the little fellow persisted. And we listened. Soon, we became accustomed to a daily account of what they ate, drank, and did in the way of activity. Finally, we were invited to an open house at school and our son amicably cautioned us to remember to seek out the gerbil cage.

We were welcomed by a very busy teacher who was surrounded by an array of parents. We found our son's desk, noted a few specially prepared assignments, then began our search for the unknown. Scrutinizing a seemingly empty aquarium, we observed bits of rubble, wood shavings, and a few strange looking balls of fuzz. Within the apparatus was another container, this one of metal. A parent, standing nearby, explained that this was the gerbils' cage and they were in their little house. Coming home, we deliberated concerning a response to our son's ultimate question, *"How did you like the gerbils?"*

One week before winter vacation, we were unexpectedly confronted by a new plan of attack. *"But Mom, the teacher says we must have a note from our parents before we are allowed to bring home the gerbils.''*

"Gerbils? Home?"

"But Mom, you don't understand. The teacher is giving away the baby gerbils. And the mother and father. The boy who brought the mother and father doesn't want them anymore, and the teacher said whoever brings her a note may have them."

"Are you breaking our pact?" I defended myself. *"When Queenie died* (our third parakeet), *I told you I needed time to recover before we have any more pets. And you agreed. One week is not enough time."*

"But Mom, you don't understand. Vacation is next week and who will feed the gerbils? Teacher says someone must bring a note before then."

On the fifth day of nagging, we began to listen. And look. We saw the earnest appeal in those large blue eyes. We knew that he loved those gerbils much as we loved him. At the end of the school day, his father came to the classroom and, together, they returned home with two additions to the family.

Later that night, I crept stealthily downstairs with visions of unsightly rodents in mind. Approaching the cage with one eye closed, I mused, *"Not bad. Almost cute. Perhaps now, I won't shriek at the sight of a mouse."*

Our son's disposition seemed to improve. No animals ever had more tender, loving care than Louise and Butter-Puff. Seemingly content. Until that fateful day. Motherly instinct caused me to utter that terrifying word.

"Sick?" my hubby defended our son. *"What do you know about gerbils?"*

"Sick," I replied. *"Louise is sick."*

"You know, dear," we tried to explain as kindly as possible to those big blue eyes. *"If we take Louise to an animal hospital, it might cost ten, even twenty dollars."*

"Well, for gosh sakes, Mom. You've spent about two hundred dollars on me!"

Dad came to the rescue by visiting a kind lady in a pet shop. He returned with new types of food, tonic and directions. We cleaned the cage (ugh!), eliminated the miniature home, and diligently sliced carrots. All, to no avail.

Lolly Pop Farm was next. Our little fellow eagerly sat next to the phone. As I cradled the receiver, the blue eyes pierced my soul. I spoke softly.

"A tumor. The woman said Louise must be very ill. If we bring her there, she'll be put to sleep."

"But Mom," he cried. "Louise might not want to go to sleep." And suddenly, as he spoke the words, he seemed to comprehend.

Early the next morning, the men of the house awakened, dressed, and ate breakfast. Louise was to be taken to Lolly Pop Farm before work and school. As I entered the kitchen, he was standing on the cellar stairway, pail in hand.

"May I see her? Will she be warm enough?" I asked. He bolted down the stairs to the cage and returned with a small piece of blue fuzz, a blanket the gerbils had created from pieces of yarn.

"This is a farewell present from Butter-Puff to Louise," he declared in a bravely disguised voice. And out the door he dashed, where father waited in the warmed-up station wagon.

An hour later, the doorbell rang and there he stood, the wistful blue eyes painfully staring at me.

"The lady told us Louise was very sick. It's a good thing we brought her there. She was in pain, Mom. We'll bring Butter-Puff tomorrow, because he'll probably be too lonesome without Louise."

Thus, the neumonen of family pets. Nuisance? Often. Delightful to observe? Usually. Companionable? Contingent on the nature of the beast. Expensive? Always. Do any survive? Rarely.

Somewheres before or after Louise and Butter-Puff, came the afore-mentioned three parakeets, several goldfish; a turtle whose back suddenly became moldy, and two dogs, Spotty and Lulu Belle. Although the latter was a male, it was discovered after the childen had named him. Thus, his name remained, until the day he became ill and was laid to rest.

How does one immunize against the painful eventualities of pet ownership? Often, during those growing up years of our family, I searched for an answer. And with it comes an apology for resorting to an outrageously conventional cliche. *Better to have loved and lost, than never to have loved at all.*

The Day We Headed South

"And now, behold, we are in thine hand: as it seemeth good and right unto thee to do unto us, do."
Joshua 9:25

Dearest Daddy,

Sundry mental images vividly remain within the framework of lifetime memories, while others are soon forgotten. Rarely, does a vibrant and gloomy remembrance surface at will, as, characteristically, I recall the day we headed south.

Until then, life had been blissfully spent in two cities within relatively short distance. We could easily visit back and forth, week after week. Year after year. College days. Married years. Lively weekends were spent together, simply, by flitting east or west on the thruway.

Later on, our homes were a few blocks apart, when we ventured back towards the family homestead, where we spent several years amongst family and childhood friends, now with families of their own. Two magical words. Friends. Family.

One day, after fifteen years of marriage, hubby decided to change our lifestyle. Often, discontent husbands imbibe as a solution. Other dudes, indicating a sense of mystery, ingratiate themselves with frivolous, young maidens. My husband? He merely wished to begin a new business venture in a tropical climate. Did I complain? Vociferously!

Returning home from the first fall day of teaching in a country school district, I was ecstatic.

"Love the job," I exclaimed. *"Best music position ever. Kids are terrific. Lots of wonderful materials. Great scene."*

"That's nice, honey. Good thing, because today, I quit my job." Turning several shades of red, I began to voice an opinion in shrill, soniferous tones.

Early each morning, when I left, hubby adapted an exciting new schedule. After taking the children to school, he and a buddy met for a coffee clotch. Totally relaxed, they plotted their destinies over a cup of coffee. Or two. Or three.

"Enough of that," I intoned one day, a few weeks later. *"Have you given anymore thought to the possibility of a new career? What was that, you say? You're disconsolate? Dejected? So, who's happy?"*

A huge package arrived the following week.

"What is that?" I asked, glancing at cans and more cans that were labeled *vinyl spray*.

"I'm going into business," my car salesman of eighteen years replied.

"You're what?"

"Going into business. It's a vinyl repair venture. Can't lose."

"So easy," the magazine ad promised. Of course. Simple. Just like everything in life. Right? Wrong! Soon, my handsome, vinyl repairman with the green eyes, was on his way to California. A brief course at vinyl repair school.

"This will solve everything," he smilingly assured as he waved goodbye.

"Having a great time here in California, honey," he wrote on a pretty picture postcard. *"Visiting with old friends. Great place, California."*

Hopefully, he'd come home to his wife and three children.

And home he came. *"Must rent a store for the business,"* he whispered one day, in barely audible tone.

"Great! And what do you plan to use for money?" I smartly quipped.

So it continued, daily. Week to week. One morning, we awakened to a magnificent snowfall, now three feet high. But oh, so picturesque. That first snowfall of the season leaves one with a feeling of quietly blissful anticipation. Of more to come.

Hubby plowed his way to work that day, lighting the heater in his little shop. Arriving home towards evening, he seemed to be ebullient with good news. We anxiously waited as he began to speak, grinning from ear to ear. Could it be? Had he received a large contract?

"How would you like to move to Florida?"

"Florida? Florida! Are you out of your mind?" I chided in a most uncomplimentary voice.

"Why on earth should we want to move to Florida? Everything we desire is right here."

"But honey, listen. When I went into this business, they didn't tell me the chemicals would freeze up in a cold climate. How was I to know? Now, I've got everything going, all set. All I need is a warm climate in which to operate," hubby pleaded.

Meditating on how settled our lives had become, I pictured the warm, spring, Sunday morning bicycle rides to you and Mama for breakfast. A few moments in the opposite direction to kid brother, sister-in-law and baby nephews. Or, the delightful knock at the door and Daddy's smiling face, arms laden with bags of goodies for the children. Up jumped the dog, grabbing at the slice of meat thrown into the air for him to catch. Such a welcome sight. And so constant. Meeting a cousin on a busy street corner. More relatives than one could comfortably recollect. All within easy grasp.

Older brother and his family were within a weekend's

easy reach. And his lament that would long be remembered, *"You're breaking up the family."* How would we ever manage to leave all these riches?

The following June, when the children finished school, the family automobile headed for Florida.

"Just to look around," he said. The old car, dragging a heavy trailer, heated up every few miles. Kids shrieking. Dog barking. Motor blowing up. Wife screaming. What a sight. And finally, the arrival.

A word of wisdom. Never rent an apartment sight unseen. We did. *"Clean, luxurious two bedroom apartment on the ocean,"* read the ad. To the omission of one simple item.

"Roaches? How dare you accuse me of having roaches in my apartments?" she vehemently asked, eyes glaring.

Most aggravating dilemmas have a positive aspect. Thus, I became an 'early-to-bedder', jumping in next to hubby as soon as he retired each evening. No late night refrigerator raids. A simple manner in which to lose unwanted pounds. For, I truly did not wish to compete with the large family of vermin we had as housemates.

After two torturous weeks, we headed for the state's west coast. Trailer parked in an attractive recreational area, several days were spent in researching the city, whereupon, we suddenly found ourselves nodding affirmatively to the sales ploy of a condominium dweller.

Less than two weeks later, our venerable *FOR SALE* sign perched on the front lawn, the doorbell rang and I stood facing a much endeared teacher from high school days. She and hubby talked and, within the month, finally agreed to the sale of our beautiful home.

One moment, the daydream. Sunny Florida. No more snow to shovel. No more bitter cold weather and icicles crashing from the roof-top. No more icy roads to travel on early school mornings.

Then, just as suddenly, a well of tears, the tale of woe lamented to friends.

"Lord, help me endure this burdensome time in my life. How can we leave Mama and Daddy? The family? Our dear ones?" I silently prayed, as the weeks quickly passed in preparation for the immense transference of our lives.

It was the first week in November. Early one morning, a moving van appeared at the door. Goodbyes were said to the Cunninghams and Bicks, choice neighbors of total endearment, whose cozy homes rested on either side. Patrick, with button nose pressed against the window, waved to the children each morning, as they left for school. Now, staring in wonder, he sadly waved for the last time.

Mama prepared dinner that final night and we sat, morosely chewing our food, paying little attention to its succulent taste.

"The Torah says," you began, trying to inject a cheerful tone into your voice. *"The Torah says that when a woman marries, her husband becomes of first importance and her parents second."*

"Ah, Daddy, that really makes me feel better," I attempted to reply in lighthearted tones.

After spending a sleepless night, we awakened early the next morning.

"Lord, help me to be strong," the words rang over and over in my mind. It was thus far, after all, perhaps the first distasteful task I'd had to encounter in life. And now, for the vibrantly gloomy mental image about which this tale began.

On that bitterly cold, dark morning, we marched, one by one, the length of the living room, headed for the front door. Bidding farewell for the final time, we climbed into the automobile, deceptive smiles on each face. You and Mama stood behind the storm door.

As always, you were dressed, even on that early morning, in a dark suit. But, most of all, I treasure the memory of your hat. You had on the businessman's derby, ready to go to work. Mama, in her housedress, managed a limp smile as you both waved in optimistic pretense. When I am old and gray and hunched with age, I shall still recall you and Mama, standing in that doorway.

Turn Around

*"Turn Thou us unto Thee,
O Lord, and we shall be
turned;
Renew our days as of old."*
 Lamentations 5:21

Dearest Daddy,

    There are moments in life when a thought, a glance, triggers the mind and we reflect on what was special and beautiful. The strangeness of it all, to realize the actual experience was not as profound as the memory it creates.

    On that day several years ago, when I arrived at your apartment to assist with packing, you and Mama were anticipating the move to a new condominium. Mama was not well and you were desperately attempting to make her feel better, more content.

    Mama decided to sort dresser drawers. We sat on the carpet, opening one drawer at a time. Examining a tissue wrapped package, our eyes met with a delicate, meticulously knit infant's ensemble, done in exquisite pastels. I had never seen the outfit and Mama had not looked at it for years. Evidently, it had remained carefully wrapped for decades.

    Mama's face held a faint smile, then the pain and anguish of realization became apparent. With a sudden flood of tears, she cried out. Where had the years gone? Had they blindly disappeared? Mama embraced the outfit she had knit for your firstborn son.

    She began to recall the happiness of those early years, when there was so much to which you looked forward. The intense blessing of parenthood. The years had been permeated with richness, as you both strived to provide a warm and loving home for your growing family. Abundance of wealth steeped in tradition. Rewards and concerns of raising three children. Memories became vivid. In that brief moment, Mama wept for fifty years that had passed. One slow motion turn of the camera. And it was . . . gone.

We held each other closely for a few seconds. Never before, had I felt so endeared to Mama, as at that moment. An instantaneous flash of discernment. As though, suddenly, I had learned the meaning of life.

Cantor Paul Niederland and the Temple Beth El Choir
"SINGING PRAISES" - Circa 1970.

Marriage Certificate

כתובה

This Is To Certify

That on the 6th day of the week, the 12th day of the month _Adar I_ in the year 57_19_ corresponding to the _19_ day of _Feb._, 19_59_, the holy Covenant of Marriage was entered into, in _Rochester, N.Y._ between the Bridegroom _Harry M. Stein_ and his Bride _Arlene Cohen_

The said Bridegroom made the following declaration to his Bride: "Be thou my wife according to the law of Moses and of Israel. I faithfully promise that I will be a true husband unto thee. I will honor and cherish thee; I will work for thee; I will protect and support thee, and will provide all that is necessary for thy due sustenance, even as it becomes a Jewish husband to do. I also take upon myself all such further obligations for thy maintenance as are prescribed by our religious statute."

And the said Bride has plighted her troth unto him, in affection and sincerity, and has thus taken upon herself the fulfilment of all the duties incumbent upon a Jewish wife.

This Covenant of Marriage was duly executed and witnessed this day according to the usage of Israel.

Rabbi   _Witnesses_

"OUR WEDDING" Certificate

The Certificate in Hebrew

Mr. and Mrs. Moe Cohen
request the honour of your presence
at the marriage of their daughter
Arlene
to
Mr. Harry M. Stein
Thursday, February nineteenth
Nineteen hundred and fifty-nine
at six-thirty o'clock
Beth Sholom Congregation
1101 Monroe Avenue
Rochester, New York

Arlene Cohen and Harry Melville Stein - February 19, 1959.
"OUR WEDDING"

The bride with Mama and Daddy.
"OUR WEDDING"

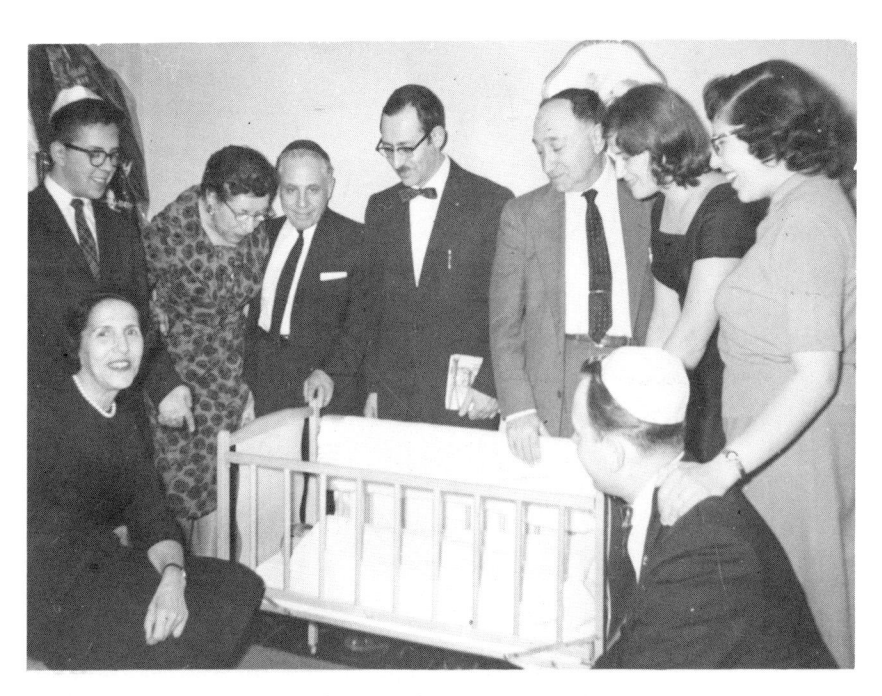

Brit Milah of Louis William Stein - March 25, 1960.
L. to R. Fanny Niederland, Eugene, Mama, Daddy, Rabbi Ginsberg,
Cantor Niederland, Shirley, Arlene, Harry.
"THE BRIHS"

Grandpa Moe with Louis and Howard. 1963.
"PASTRAMI ON RYE AND APPLE STRUDEL"

Grandpa Moe and Grandma Mae with Louis, Howard and Sherri, 1964.
"PASTRAMI ON RYE AND APPLE STRUDEL"

"UNION STATION"

Passover Seder 1961.
Daddy conducts our Seders.
"CHANUKAH, PURIM AND PASSOVER"

Passover Seder 1961.

Passover Seder 1966.

Passover Seder 1968.

Passover Seder 1975.

Louis, Howard and Sherri. Circa 1969.
"PRECIOUS JEWELS PRICELESS FEEDBACK"

Arlene, Harry and Family. 1986.
"PRECIOUS JEWELS PRICELESS FEEDBACK"

Louis William's
Bar Mitzvah. 1973.
"BAR MITZVAHS"

Howard Alan's
Bar Mitzvah. 1976.
"BAR MITZVAHS"

Grandpa Moe and Grandma Mae at Howard's Bar Mitzvah party. 1976.
"BAR MITZVAHS"

Our home on Brighton Place - Circa 1971.
"THE DAY WE HEADED SOUTH"

Our home on South Brink Avenue.
1978 - 1990.
Where Daddy conducted his last Seder.
**"CHANUKAH, PURIM
AND PASSOVER"**

Mama and Daddy's last photo together.
November 1981.
"SUDDEN DEATH AND BROKEN TIES"

Stuart, Syril, Aunt Aurelia,
Doris, Arlene and Herbert.
Maternal Cousins. 1936.

Sherri and Milton.
Paternal Cousins.
1986.

Lucy and Mark.
Paternal Cousins.
Circa 1965.

"WHERE HAVE ALL THE COUSINS GONE?"

Mama, Lilly Guy (holding Arlene on her lap), her sister, Fige, Bill,
their daughter, Syril, son, Stuart and Herbert. Maternal Cousins. 1936.

Henny and Sam Greene, Doris and Leonard Singer, Mamie Sugerman-Rosenblum, Ed and Lilly Guy, Arlene. 1991.

Mamie and Henny 1992.

Aunt Aurelia, Uncle Dick with daughter, Barbara and two grandchildren, Scott & Mathew. Circa 1982.

'The Two Aurelias' Lilly (Aurelia) Guy and Aurelia Lippman

'Three sisters' Lilly Guy, Evelyn Cooperman and Mamie Sugerman-Rosenblum. Circa 1989.

"WHERE HAVE ALL THE COUSINS GONE?"

A smattering of maternal cousins.

Arlene, Ellen and Gail.
Maternal and Paternal Cousins.
Circa 1954.

Judy and Lois
Paternal Cousins. 1953.

"WHERE HAVE ALL THE COUSINS GONE?"

Reva, Sherri, Susan, Ruth Ann,
Michael, Linda,
Paternal Cousins. 1965.

Billy and Barbara.
Maternal Cousins. 1952.

"WHERE HAVE ALL THE COUSINS GONE?"

Joe and Inez Jacobs and Sadie and Sam Baum.
Maternal Cousins. Circa 1970-'73.

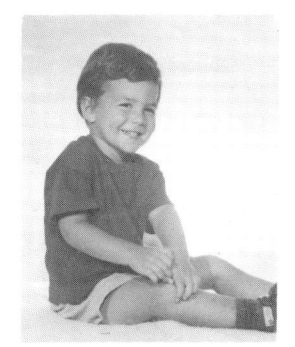

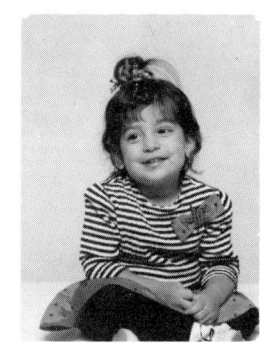

Sophie and Stanley Rothstein. Circa 1945 - '47.
Their grandchildren. Circa 1990. Maternal Cousins

Jenny Kamino, Gert Peretz, Sylvia and Judge Herald Hymes.
Circa 1973. Paternal Cousins.

A smattering of cousins, at our wedding. 1959.
"WHERE HAVE ALL THE COUSINS GONE?"

Debbie and Mathew. Maternal Cousins.
Circa 1986.

"RABBI LAZER"
and his family. 1990

The Attic

"So teach us to number our days, that we may apply our hearts unto wisdom."
Psalms 90:12

Dearest Daddy,

No place fills one with an aura of mystery and sense of romance, like the attic of a home. Poetic verses have oft been written about that haunting, upper room. Writers of murder mysteries plant evidence, even their culprits, in the garret of a home.

By means of the attic on Leslie Avenue, you and Mama provided us with a pictorial diary of your lives. That hot, summer day remains ever clear in my mind. The summer following our move south, you decided to sell our homestead. The children and I took the long train ride on AMTRAK, heading back to Leslie Avenue for the last time. You and Mama prepared to initiate an enormous change in your lives. We were filled with a strange sense of sadness, as we anticipated leaving the only home we truly remembered. We were, however, sustained by the thought that you and Mama, once again, would soon be living nearby, in a southern residence. During several telephone conversations, I assured Mama that the children and I would supervise an expansive garage sale during the course of our visit.

The air was thick and humid as I climbed the stairway to the attic. The garage was already filled with dozens of unique objects, furniture and bric-a-brac. Mama and her two visiting grandchildren directed traffic and promoted sales. I had decided to explore the attic for more items to contribute to the sale. Although clad in nothing but a pair of shorts and halter, the sweat began dripping in all directions, as I searched carton after carton. Filled with astonishment, my mind frantically wandered from decade to decade. Soon, I was not sure where the sweat subsided and tears began.

There was so much to see, to remember. Boxes of scrapbooks, pictures, school projects, report cards. From first grade through college. Letters. Cards. Tons and tons of greeting cards. Cards you and Mama had given each other, even before marriage. Valentines, birthday cards, anniversary cards. Cards received upon the birth of your children. Cards of silk. Puffy, three-dimensional hearts. Then, suddenly, cards and notes of sympathy sent to Mama upon the death of her father, my grandfather, Aaron. It filled me with a sense of sadness and awe to read of the death of a grandfather I had never known, but, with whom I had always felt a special affinity. During his lifetime, hardly more than half a century, he allowed only one picture to be taken. After Mama's mother died, a skilled photographer combined two separate snap-shots, creating a formal portrait of our maternal grandparents. Now, many years later, as I read the notes, this inadvertently forsaken grandparent entered my life once more.

There were letters from Uncle Yunk, Mama's brother, nicknamed Utta by his nephew, who, as a toddler, could not pronounce the word, uncle. During World War II, Yunk's letters came from China, where he was stationed with the army. I wrote him about thunder and lightening storms during our summer hiatus at Sylvan Beach, and he replied, crowning me with glorious praise as his most loyal correspondent. It was the summer of my ninth birthday.

Tired at last, from crouching on my heels, I stood and slowly began taking in the surroundings. Deeply engrossed in the cartons, I had neglected to look at the larger pieces in the attic. On one side, stood the ornately carved maple wood crib in which we had all slept. I laughed inwardly, as I recalled the years spent in that crib. At the age of six and in first grade, I climbed from that crib each morning, to prepare for school. Evidently, you and Mama saw no need to purchase a bed, until the birth of our younger brother. It became a family joke, asking ourselves how long I might have remained in the crib, if not for the arrival of another sibling.

Slipcovers and draperies. There they lay, neatly folded and wrapped in large sheets of tissue paper. The bold floral design on pale blue background, called to mind those years of long ago, when Mama sweated and labored each spring. Mama's *spring cleaning* was so much more. It meant re-decorating, especially the living and dining room. Slipcovers were fitted to chairs and sofa. New draperies, richly colorful, hung at the windows. Simply by virtue of these changes, our faith in life was renewed, filling us with an unusual sense of happiness and well-being.

Lamps. There they stood. Green alabaster base, long graceful brass arms reaching up to two silk shades. Another mini-floor lamp, its brass appendage curved to the socket, also surrounded by a silk shade. I remembered. Mama's bridge lamp. How many years since it had graced our living room?

Then suddenly, a large black trunk. Careful not to trip as I reached, sweat dripping over my eyes, I knelt before this treasure. Slowly, I opened it. Oh, truly, this was more than I had imagined! Our dancing costumes! My fingers caressed the sequins and satin as I envisioned the stage. At the age of five, I had tapped my way to local fame on the stage of the Stanley Theater. All that remained of my brief dancing career was a formal portrait of a smiling little girl, posing on one bended knee, right arm upward, black patent tap shoes, blue and white costume shorts, white hat, decorated with red pom poms. Two long, dark brown curls traveled the length of the costume.

Big brother and I had taken lessons at Mr. Burlow's dance studio. Brother's white satin, long-sleeved dancing blouse lay with my costume in the trunk.

Suddenly, I heard voices below. Our younger son was calling, *"Mom, come on down and help us. Grandma wants to know how much to ask for the orange planter."* That lovely old, orange wicker plant holder with its long legs. How we fancied setting it on the porch each spring. It had a matching table on which we played with our paper dolls. Shirley, Tweezie, Cornelia and I. How many years ago?

"Come on, Mom. We need you. Hurry up!"

Pressing down the cover of the trunk, I tried to rise from my knees. My feet had fallen asleep. Darn! How I hated that tingling sensation! I stared out the window of the attic, where I could see Leslie Avenue. Children were playing ball on the sidewalk across from our house. Now and then, a child dashed into the road to retrieve his ball.

"Mom . . . Mom! Come help with the garage sale." I prayed inwardly. *"Please God, help time to pass less quickly."*

The Minyan

*"Every day will I bless Thee:
And I will bless Thy name
For ever and ever."*
Psalms 145:2

Dearest Daddy,

Since your departure, days have quickly passed into weeks. Soon, eleven months of reciting mourners' kaddish will end. The greatest revelation during this period, was achieved by my presence at morning minyan.

Innumerable hours are spent in synagogue. Shabat. Holy Days. Year unto year; decade after decade. Yet, little is witnessed concerning the core, the very heart of our religion, our heritage. The daily minyan. On a weekday morning, entering synagogue is an experience unique from any other aspect of Judaism.

When Mama died, it was naturally assumed that you and your sons shared responsibility incumbent upon males; recital of kaddish. However, shortly after your departure, I sensed within, a deep awakening. Early one morning, a few weeks later, I stood at the door of the sanctuary.

Glancing towards the front as I entered, I became fascinated by the sight of more than a dozen male constituents of the synagogue. Beneath a yarmulka, the skullcap worn by several religious sects, black leather straps enveloped each head. The straps continued downward, according to custom, encircling the left arm, neatly ending around the fingers. Several men turned as they davened, many, reciting familiar prayers from memory. A square black box, perhaps an inch in size, rested on each forehead, between the eyes; one similar, on the left arm. These phylacteries or tefillin are, symbolically, worn by Orthodox or Conservative men during morning prayer on weekdays.

"You shall bind them for a sign upon your hand, and they shall be for frontlets between your eyes."

How many years had those words from Deuteronomy been recited during attendance at services?

In the weeks that followed, I mused concerning the lives of those who attended morning services. What compelled them to come? Was it for some, a true spiritual endeavor, religious affirmation to God? For others, a traditional habit? Yet, for many, simply a social activity? For whatever reason, came the sudden realization that the minyan was the very essence of Judaism. Without daily, or as in the case of increasing numbers of congregations, at very least, a twice weekly occurrence of minyanim, our faith was becoming rapidly diluted.

Male cohorts were solicitous, evidently, unaccustomed to the presence of women during the morning minyan. For centuries, the presence of ten men was required to constitute a minyan or quorum. Certain prayers remained unspoken, unless the requisite number was present. Recently, the conservative movement had adapted the custom of calling female members to the bimah or pulpit. Occasionally, mutterings could be heard by a few men, who, unhappily, adhered to the new practice. Yet, few women gave thought to the possibility of being included. Each time I entered the sanctuary, I prayed that there would already be a male quorum. With respect to our heritage, I have no desire to actively engage in women's liberation.

Occasionally, another feme was quietly seated nearby. It was always someone observing Yahrzeit, the annual commemoration of a loved one's death. Aside from those infrequent moments, I remained the sole female attendee of the morning minyan.

A feeling of sanctity is imposed upon one who practices this ritual. Perhaps, the early morning hour lends itself to a more sacred environment than exists during other moments. Friday evenings have become weekly social gatherings in the majority of temples. When questioned, individuals admittedly reply that they enjoy socializing, scrutinizing the latest in wearing apparel, and evaluating refreshments served at the *Oneg Shabat,* the reception following the service.

Moreover, when a Bar or Bat Mitzvah takes place, an additional source of pleasure is provided. Further judgment is passed on floral arrangements, types of food and beverage served, and size, color and height of helium balloons. Our grandparents would be aghast were they ever to witness such an event. We ask our sons and daughters to achieve religious maturity, as we confront them with frivolity symbolic of fools.

The morning minyan reminded me of the promises of our forefathers. The joy and holiness of our heritage is evident in the series of psalms and prayers recited. There is no indication of mourning in the mourner's kaddish. It is, rather, a statement of life, speaking of the glory of God, life's goodness and desire of peace for mankind.

Judaism is a practical religion. If we explore traditional rules, we learn there are prayers for almost every move we make. Likewise, within the daily minyan, different prayers are recited for Rosh Chodesh, the first day of the Hebrew month; for the eight days of Chanukah; for the month preceding High Holy Days; for Chol Hamoed, the intermediary days of Passover and Succoth. And so, on and on.

I quickly recognized my sparsity of knowledge. I wondered why never before, had I felt the desire to avail myself of the morning minyan. I became aware of a great paradox, the clever ideology promoted by our ancestors.

Survivors bear responsibility for coming to synagogue for nearly a year, following the death of a parent or close family member. Thus perhaps, parental failure of achievement during life, is attained after one's death. Daily minyan services, chock full of tradition, serve to inspire unfaithful participants, as they mourn their loved ones. On the other hand, our sages provided us with prayers to alleviate the stress.

I felt the blood rushing to head and heart as I read, *"I kept faith even when I was greatly afflicted. When, unthinking, I condemned all life as vain."* The Psalms were beautiful to read. Then, Chronicles was before me. *"Strength and courage come from You; Greatness and power are Your gifts."*

How could one read these words and not find solace? Daddy, I pictured you, as you once were, the mainstay of these minyanim. The Rabbi had aptly expressed it when he told me that echoes of your masterful davenen continued to reverberate in Shul, unheard, but sweet. Indeed, so true.

Often, upon entering the synagogue, inwardly, I heard your voice as you once lead the services. Minyanim continue from generation to generation. They are our link with the past, present and future. A veritable heritage bequeathed to us by our father, his father, and his father's father. And so it shall be.

Bar Mitzvahs

"And thou shalt bind them for a sign upon thy hand, and they shall be for frontlets between thine eyes.
Deuteronomy 6:8

Dearest Daddy,

The tumult has subsided. That long-awaited simcha, day of joy, has come and gone. It was special in many ways, and for manifold reasons. You were here when the date was set, but, deep within, was a sense of foreboding.

Fourteen years earlier, we had rejoiced at the Bat Mitzvah of your firstborn grandchild. Then came Louis, whose innocent discernment proclaimed him firstborn grandson and prime Bar Mitzvah. In short order, appeared a second grandson, then Howard, and two more. Each occasion, a time for great celebration. Sometime between Sherri's twelfth and thirteenth year, we endowed her with the honor of life membership in Hadassah, whereby Mama received a handsome, gold three-generation pin. In accordance with earlier generations, our decision to gloss over her Bat Mitzvah, was based on the Orthodox tradition that precluded a ceremony for female siblings, but in recent years, has been encouraged even amongst these strict adherents.

Often, both you and Mama remarked in semi-serious manner, *"We'll probably not be here for the youngest grandsons' Bar Mitzvahs."* The biological clock was ticking, and time, that heartless scoundrel, bestowed grandsons whose Bar Mitzvahs remained several years away.

When Sherri made her first trip to Israel, she was instructed with the intricacies of procuring a tallit, the prayer shawl. Each grandson had received the special gifts of our heritage from Grandpa Moe, during study for the Bar Mitzvah.

Sherri returned with a beautiful, pale blue tallit. Your tefillin, the phylacteries acquired during young manhood, had been sent to Israel with a friend, and were restored, awaiting use by their young servant

You shall bind them as a sign upon your hand; they shall be as frontlets between your eyes. One can't help but wonder if these words truly reach the heart and mind of a thirteen year old boy as he commences with tradition. We put our children through the motions. They obey. Do they comprehend? *These words which I command you this day shall be in your heart. You shall teach them diligently to your children.*

Your heart was filled with these commandments. Your diligence and Mama's, so great as you taught your children. Indeed, our family lived by these traditions. We did not have to learn about them at synagogue. They were ever present in our home. Most friends had similar guidelines. Although, admittedly, our home was amongst the richest in traditions, we were not singled out as being unique.

And so as we entered the temple for that final Bar Mitzvah, we walked down the aisle to the front row. Seated, I closed my eyes, whereupon, I became enveloped with a strange sensation. I was sitting next to Mama and she smiled, that soft smile filled with the happiness and pride we had often observed. I saw you standing at the bimah, towards the side, eyes studying the words of the Torah. There you remained, next to your grandson throughout the entire ceremony.

Sudden Death And Broken Ties

"Man is like unto a breath; His days are as a shadow that passeth away."
     Psalms 144.4

Dearest Daddy,

Today was my fiftieth birthday, a truly formidable moment in one's life. Celebration began on Fourth of July in niece, Linda's apartment. During the next three days, it persisted, with jubilant homage on the part of would-be wellwishers. Until, at last, came that moment of actuality, the time of my birth on the seventh day of the seventh month.

Most assuredly, I thought of you and Mama. Birthdays in our family had always been favored with strong feelings of togetherness. So difficult now, since you and Mama departed.

When a woman reaches her thirtieth, then fortieth birthdays, she still imagines herself as part of a glamorous world. The number fifty however, has inelegant connotations, especially since it causes one to realize how quickly life on earth passes.

Memories came to mind as I celebrated my half century of life. One does not think about birth without contemplating death. Visions took hold as I remembered the quick, simple manner in which both you and Mama had bid us farewell. Death always comes too rapidly. Yours and Mama's were most traditional.

That night, when Mama sat quietly upward, tensed beneath the headboard of the hospital bed, she evidently sensed what was about to happen. No sound emitted as she gazed motionless, tears dropping to her cheeks. Nurses hurriedly placed a surgical cap on her head, as a narrow bed was wheeled into the room. It was to be a *minor surgical procedure*. In less than an hour, they assured her family, Mama would return to her room, feeling well once more. Quickly, they wheeled her down the hallway as we followed, thoughts of apprehension removed from our minds as we spoke words of encouragement.

Embarrassment veiled our fear, as each one timidly felt Mama's hand before entering a nearby waiting room. I stood, while two nurses impatiently attended, as though a fire siren had sounded and we must leave the building as quickly as possible. Was this minor surgical procedure so vital that each second remained crucial to Mama's well-being? Reflections cause one to wonder. It was late evening. Perhaps, it was moments from the time when these nurses changed shifts, making this a final duty for the night.

Ah, yes. It was quite final when I quickly embraced Mama and, as cheerfully as possible, told her not to worry. We were waiting in a little room across the hall and would see her soon. Mama never spoke a word to us as we bid farewell. She knew. Yes, she knew.

Lapsing into a coma, Mama remained alive for several hours after the *minor surgery,* as we tortured ourselves with useless questions. Her journey of life was complete. She had reached her destination. Yet, what had happened to those final moments for which we often plan? The soothing words we know we'll speak? What of the worthy endeavors dreamed, but not yet executed? Uncelebrated occasions at which we hoped to rejoice and to which we looked forward? A foolish minor surgical procedure and it was over. One ponders intense thoughts; questions for which there are no answers.

Two years and six months later, our dear father would also deny his family the process of a seemly farewell. It began suddenly, one morning, with that severe lower back pain. As one thing led to another, you finally succumbed to pressure from physician and family, agreeing to spend several days in the hospital. We breathed sighs of relief, realizing you would be strengthened, albeit momentarily, by having three square meals according to schedule. In addition, we ceased worrying about whether or not you were turning a mattress or scrubbing the kitchen floor on hands and knees. Areas of housekeeping in which you happily excelled.

Several days later, you convinced the doctor you were well enough to return home. With dire concern, I hired the help necessary to attend to your needs during the absence of loved ones. It was a rapidly declining physical breakdown, happening before our very eyes. Medication and hours spent at concocting traditional home remedies, did not seem to help.

By the end of the week, having suffered a heart attack, we spoke lighthearted words as you lay in intensive care, midst tubular connections. Neither you, nor I, were ready to admit by conversation, that final moments were rapidly approaching. We had spent so many hours during the last two years thinking optimistic thoughts, when the odds were against us. Father and daughter, both spirited and headstrong, conversing in detail about problems that assailed loved ones. Better times would come, we assured ourselves. Always, with that air of confidence, we seemed to console one another.

We spent that final hour whispering useless idioms to which we were accustomed when fear loomed imminent. However you might have felt, I waxed optimism, ever hopeful that you would soon recover. I left with the promise to return several hours later with homemade soup.

It was nearly six o'clock. The soup was heated almost

to boiling point, the way you liked it. An uneasy feeling enveloped me as I hastened to pour it into a large cup. I was seized with a sudden urge to telephone the intensive care unit. Why was I nervous? No more than three minutes from the hospital, I would soon be at your side. Why call?

A nurse answered the telephone. *"How is my father doing?"* I asked, suddenly overcome with dread. *"He just this minute began to have difficulties. They are working over him now. Please come immediately."*

I screamed into the receiver. *"Why didn't you call me?"*

"Please understand, it just happened. We were going to call you," she impatiently replied.

Suddenly, the idea of homemade split pea soup seemed ridiculous. I raced from the kitchen to the car. Emotions were at an all time high. My world began to collapse. Slowly. Then, with rapid heaviness. The pain and torture were once more evident. Fear. Such panic. Emptiness. A hollow feeling deep within. And we never even said goodbye.

Precious Jewels
Priceless Flashback

*"... for consider how great
things he hath done for you."*
I. Samuel 12:24

Dearest Daddy,

Safely tucked away in a secret corner, is the small brown jewelry case that was given to Mama during our growing up years. Lined with plushy, dark green velvet material, each tiny compartment is enfolded in soft luxury. *"How can one little box contain such a vast assortment of memorabilia?"* I wonder, gazing at the collection of trinkets and precious jewelry. No matter how great or small the monetary value in terms of the now period in our lives, each adornment is a gem with a story to tell.

Slowly opening the zippered pocket of a miniature pink satin case, I am rewarded by the sight of several rings. Two unseemingly thin circlets are an instant reminder of Mama's mother, Sarah Freidel, the grandma who lived with us for a short period of time. The engagement ring, minus its diamond, calls to mind that fateful June morning almost four decades earlier. When you left Buba's bedside at the nursing home where she resided, there was a definite awareness of both wedding band and engagement ring, with the tiny diamond flashing in the darkness. Now, several hours later, standing at her side, where she lay in final stillness, her children were shocked by the vacant little setting on the betrothal band. The missing stone in Buba's ring gave credence to rumors that diamonds could easily be sequestered by those who had no conscience.

Returning Buba's rings to their compartment, I gaze upon a five-pointed star atop a small cluster of diamonds. Yielding to the common factor of *middle age*, I remove my eyeglasses to see the detail. Each point of the star is glazed in a different color. The cluster of diamonds proves to be five more miniature stars, each centered with a tiny diamond. This was Mama's Eastern Star ring.

Reflecting on a day several decades past, I visualize two little girls strolling down Oneida Street. Ahead of us, walked Mama with the mother of Jackie, my friend. The ladies chatted happily, as they went about the business of promoting the good deeds of Eastern Star.

Often, on a weekday evening, Mama dressed in the softly flowing white gown. A lovely sight to behold, her steel gray hair was curled to perfection, lips painted an enhancing shade of red with matching curved nails adorning those long, slender fingers on graceful hands. The ring was always worn on the little finger of her right hand, and now, I noted the matching pin in the velvety folds of the jewelry box. Attached on a silver chain, was a diminutive gavel, awarded at the close of her year of stardom as Shoshano Chapter's matron.

With outstanding leadership, both you and Mama had imbued innumerable friends and acquaintances of the community. While Mama held the gavel, you served as chancellor commander of your lodge. As young children, we sensed the significance of the surrounding tumult. Hidden in a drawer of the old secretary desk, are boxes of index cards containing memorable speeches rehearsed during the wee hours of night. Now, long years later, I study the mysterious nature of these organizations, once considered an intrusion upon privacy. Yet, I read with wonder and delight. Such a pity that these eloquent speeches were kept for designated ears. I study Mama's rhetoric concerning the wonders of living in her beloved, adoptive country. Patriotism. Recalling our heritage. Familial devotion. *"Why, oh why?"* I ask myself. How did one write such beautiful words, only to be kept for a select few?

Reaching into the satin bag, I remove an exquisite, delicately carved cameo ring, its rectangular shape jarring my mind. The ring of innermost secret desires. Hardly worn by Mama at the time of my tenth year, I muse at the probability of why. Lately, my wedding band is reluctantly squeezed up, up, up, where once, it easily found its way. *"Fluid or flesh?"* we ask. Then, one day, we no longer bother.

This little beauty, cameo on one side, held an exciting surprise. It was reversible. With a push and a click, the opposite side displayed a black onyx topped by a diamond. Whenever Mama asked me to dust her dresser, I found the charming ring housed in a tiny case. One quick look until the next time.

In the upper berth of the little jewelry box, sits an old wrist watch, minus a band. The round, bold face is a sight for tired eyes. Large, distinctive, no-nonsense numbers are painted in bright gold. No need to guess about the time and who cares about the day or date? One can glance at a calendar. Please, please, just give us the time. Small letters spell the word, Elgin. I turn the wind-up on the side. For heaven's sake, it actually works. The moments tick away as I visualize it resting on Daddy's wrist countless years ago. He and Mama were young parents and we were but fledglings.

After selecting a small gold pendant, its thin lines surrounding a diamond that hangs by a gold thread, I quickly race to the portrait of Mama's parents hanging on a nearby wall. Buba stares back as I note with delight, the necklace adorning her. A pendant given to her by our grandfather, a rare treasure among their extremely few possessions.

The largest item in the box awaiting inspection, I

remove a thick-chained gold bracelet. I recall that day during my early bridal years, when Mama and I went shopping. Mama had decided she would like a gold bracelet on which to hang the rapidly accumulating charms designating the birth of each grandchild. One by one, she welcomed the little gold silhouettes and had them soldered to the bracelet. Within a decade plus half, Mama had nine little charms hanging on the gold bracelet. Silhouettes of two granddaughters and seven grandsons.

A small, hexagon shape gold charm is engraved with words announcing a thirtieth anniversary. And in the center of Mama's exquisite wrist ornament is the largest charm of all. Circular, surrounded by gold braid, a bride and groom are encompassed by two stones. Above and below the couple, are the words, *Happy Anniversary*. On the reverse side, loving words and the date signify your fiftieth wedding anniversary. I recall the moment you invited my opinion concerning an appropriate gift for this auspicious occasion, and our decision to grace Mama's elegant bracelet with a magnificent charm. How special it was to Mama. This adornment, spelling in few words, the cares and concerns, happiness and somber moments of a lifetime.

The picture uppermost in mind, reflects back to a special moment of yesteryear; the eloquent celebration commemorating your half century together as husband and wife, our devoted parents, and dedicated grandparents. Reflecting upon past jubilant occasions, we felt that you and Mama would prefer a special affair, rather than a cruise or trip.

With hall rented for the grand event, caterer hired, decorations selected, invitations mailed, we spoke of nothing but the party, for weeks preceding the momentous occasion. Several professional musician friends, in collaboration with our two teenage sons, provided a band for dancing. Our classical trio performed, immediately following dinner. Formality prevailing, our big brother acted as master of ceremonies. Such pleasure for you and Mama, immensely proud of your firstborn son that special evening. On that gala night, each sibling was called upon to eulogize. Much to his chagrin, Uncle Herman, noted for a tendancy to endearingly elongate at such events, was asked to limit his speech. Both granddaughters expounded virtues of their cherished grandparents. Each guest received a fanciful brochure with superimposed photographs of you and Mama on the cover, and inside, biographical reviews of parents and siblings. Glancing back, a few months later, inwardly pleased with the results, I wondered why, on your golden-wedding night, praise for this clever creation had been acknowledged with discomfort. Now, indeed, it remains an eloquent souvenir.

Gazing once more, into the jewelry box, I notice your wrist watch, still ticking. It is mid-afternoon. Time to start dinner. Carefully, the elegant charm bracelet is laid to rest at the bottom of the velvet lining. Perhaps, one day, we'll offer these treasures to *our* grandchildren. It can't come soon enough for me. I'm getting tired.

Sunshine And Sorrow

"Sorrow is better than laughter: for by the sadness of the countenance the heart is made better."
Ecclesiastes 7:3

Dearest Daddy,

Ah, that I might explain these feelings of ambiguity that enter my mind whenever setting out to do errands. One might readily assume that traveling up the avenue on a beautiful, sunny day, should fill one's heart and mind with a deep sense of contentment. Today, everything flows at a perfect pace. There is lush greenery all around. Traffic flows. Birds are singing and youngsters happily wending their way home from school. I am elated, pleased with life and thankful for good health, friends, loved ones; the opportunity to work and experience a sense of achievement. My chest practically bursts with gratification.

Why then, this sudden attack of melancholy? Have I lost my sense of reality? Or, has it just returned? The human mind is indeed, a strange piece of equipment. Subconscious thoughts begin to invade my sense of well-being. An inner voice plays havoc with my ease of mind.

Someone asks, *"Happy? Why should you be happy? You're not supposed to feel well. Surely, you do have all these wonderful things taking hold in your life. But remember, 'they' are not with you any longer. You're here and they're there. You can not share this wonderful day with them. Face it. They're gone. You wish to tell them about the contract just received? The grand reception at which you'll soon perform? Gosh. Too bad."*

The voice continues, but, with little influence. Driving along, I still manage to sing. Then, suddenly, it succeeds. The car passes your apartment, the home where you and Mama resided. Besieged with a torrent of pain, a wave of nausea defies my efforts to remain calm. Nothing, absolutely nothing, surpasses the sadness experienced whenever catching a glimpse of the dwellings where countless hours were spent with you and Mama, during those retirement years. Certain photographs evoke mild, mixed feelings, but naught can compare to the dispirited frustration of facing those familiar abodes.

Slowly, the sunlight fades. Twilight descends upon my mind. Then, darkness. All is lost. In a fleeting moment, the buoyant heart shrivels and the mind slopes downward. From sunshine. To sorrow.

The Cycle of Life

"All go unto one place; all are of the dust, and all return to dust."
               Ecclesiastes 3:20

Dearest Daddy,

Precious moments of this day linger, as I savor the memory during these late night hours. I languor in the cozy confines of a motel room, picturing young Sara, her dark-eyed smile, tiny figure of twelve-plus years, as she received the Torah from her parents on the bimah this morning.

The service was different from any I had ever seen. As the youthful, bearded Rabbi took the pulpit, armed with guitar, he burst into Talmudic song. His deep voice filled the sanctuary, enrapturing the entire congregation. Eyes upon the handsome, statuesque figure, ears listening eagerly to his compelling voice, we were hooked. Sara's parents, who had written the service, participated with several friends and relatives who were called upon to read. Michael, her father, an ordained Rabbi, professor at the university, welcomed the congregation with warm congeniality, and offered explanatory comments during the service.

Daddy, I remember the magnetism which existed between you and Michael when he came into our family. You were especially drawn to him because he was studying to become a Rabbi. We always presumed you had a secret yearning to pursue this same direction and had, somehow, failed to do so during your life. Perhaps, Michael fulfilled this desire and you were reliving your past through him. Whenever cousin Audrey came for brief visits with her new, young husband, you soon found yourselves deeply engrossed in discussion. His admiration for you was obvious. He instinctively realized you were the family patriarch.

Now, watching him on the pulpit, administering to his younger daughter's Bat Mitzvah ceremony, I was reminded of those earlier years, when our family was blessed with simchas. My glance enveloped Audrey, her two daughters, Debbie and Sara, and her husband of nearly twenty years. I visualized her as a young girl, her vitality now, no less than in those years. The impact which she and her husband made on this small, vibrant, college town, was most apparent. Members of the diminutive congregation did not take their heritage for granted.

Sara's sweet young voice chanted the Haftorah portion with shy determination. Suddenly, the young Rabbi, who, years earlier, had been a student of Rabbi Michael, began to speak. He was lecturing on the cycle of life; its effect on every human being. Listening to his words, I was seized by a strong sensation. How could one, so young, realize the meaning of that phrase? Yet, moments before, Sara, too, had spoken about the cycle of life, quoting words gleaned from a song learned at summer camp.

I sat quietly, thinking of you and Mama, and the many, joyous occasions experienced as a family. Here we were, at another simcha, sans the presence of young Sara's great-aunt and uncle.

My eyes beheld a six-pointed star centered in a stained-glass window above the ark. When it was time to say mourners' kaddish, the Rabbi invited those who so desired, to rise and recite the words. I stood in loving memory of you, Mama and my brother, gazing at the star. Mouthing those words, I wondered about the cycle of life and its true meaning. Where had our loved ones gone? What is the soul? The spirit? What is the meaning of life? Or death? Who am I? What are we? Where is eternity? What *is* the cycle of life?

Where Have All The Cousins Gone?

"The Lord our God be with us, as he was with our fathers..."
　　　I. Kings 8:57

Dearest Daddy,

While growing up, we seemed to take for granted, the colossal number of cousins on the family tree. Since you and Mama both came from large clans, we inherited dozens of relatives once-removed, acquired a baker's dozen of first cousins from your side, and four more from Mama's family. Cousin Judy once pronounced an amazing fact. Of sixteen paternal first cousins, all have been married for well over twenty years, and, at least to date, not a single divorce! An amazing accomplishment during these times.

Mama, born in Poland, came to this country when two years old. Each parent already had several siblings living in America, all married and busily adding to the family tree. Brothers, sisters, spouses and children lived within blocks of one another. Some, perhaps a few miles away. Others gravitated towards larger cities. All kept in touch, but with some, the visits became fewer and further between.

Sometime, during my first ten years of life, Mama's two aunts, Tante Etta and Tante Molly, came to visit. One sister lived in Chicago, the other in New York; each with several children, Mama's first cousins whom we'd never met. It was a joyous occasion for our grandmother, Sarah Freidel, seeing these two sisters after so many, many years. We sat and listened as they talked about their other sisters, Tante Bayla and Tante Raisel, and their two brothers, Itzchak and Abram. All had come to America, working their way up from poverty to middle class status. It was a day-to-day existence, putting food on the table and acquiring minimal standards of life. There was neither time nor money. Nor, soon, even the slightest inclination to worry about one's siblings who lived hundreds of miles away. Long distance telephone calls were reserved for the wealthy. An occasional letter served to update the family tree. First cousins spent a lifetime visiting by birth announcements, notes and epistolary communication. Through Mama's conversations and explanations, each time a letter was received, we learned much about our aunts, uncles and cousins. Some of Mama's first cousins, however, lived nearby. Since the girls maintained a sisterly relationship, I truly thought they were Mama's sisters, and called each one aunt. Further confusion resulted, as I added their children to my list of first cousins.

Mama's cousin, Sarah, seemed to have a formal relationship with very young children. Although I addressed her sisters as Aunt Fige, Aunt Lilly, Aunt Mamie and Aunt Rivie, I felt more at ease by addressing her by her married name. Once in awhile, the doorbell rang, and there she stood, holding in her arms, large boxes. She and Mama pretended it was secret hush-hush, but I knew the boxes contained those long, stiff, peachy-orange corsets.

Your bedroom had a strange two-door entry, one opening to the dining room, the other into a hallway. By opening the doors back-to-back, a tiny cubicle was created, often used by Mama as a dressing area. The corsets were carried into the bedroom, where Mama tried them on. The long garment fit snugly underneath the bosom and had to be laced from bottom to top. It is impossible to imagine how women in those days, managed to breath. Mama always had at least two corsets, one for everyday, the other for dress-up evenings. Cousin Sarah and Mama used their corset encounters to catch up on family life. Sarah and her sisters, all living within close proximity, always attended family functions. Since these large families had an age differential, spanning more than a decade from oldest to youngest, there was, likewise, a vast age variation amongst their children, our cousins. Thus, there was a widespread assortment of cousins with whom we came in contact. At school, we often encountered a cousin from one household or another. A second-cousin once-removed, a fourth generation cousin. And so it went.

It became absolutely impossible to keep track of the dozens and dozens of cousins stemming from our forefathers. It also became a family joke. When engaging in conversation with a friend for merely a few moments, we'd heartily relate, *"Of course, I know him. He's my cousin."* When we married, brothers and I created mass confusion for our perplexed mates. *"Hey, Mom,"* our younger son asked one day. *"Do you think we have at least one cousin in every state?"*

"Then, Mom, why don't we try to figure out how many cousins we really have and where they live?" Somberly, I mused about the family tree I'd always planned to do. The annual family reunions spoken of more than two decades ago. Engaged in our own little private existence, we barely made the effort to be in touch with nieces, nephews, a handful of first cousins, a cousin or two, once-removed. Occasionally, we heard from a long-lost cousin, with whom we reminisced and made promises to keep in touch.

Sometime soon, I promise myself, I'll take time-out to answer the question about which I often dream. Where have all the cousins gone?

Concerts and Recitals

"Sing unto the Lord, all the earth; Proclaim His salvation from day to day."
First Chronicles 16:23

Dearest Daddy,

It is impossible to verbally express the sense of despondency sustained, since you and Mama are no longer present at our concerts. It is as though an arm were severed, yet, I foolishly hope that time will lessen the intensity of pain. I realize I shall, never again, experience the joy, at the finale of a concert, as I glanced upward to see the prideful look on your faces.

Since you left, a strange thing has occurred. When Mama was no longer with us, you nobly carried on. At first, when you attended our musical events, you cried in evident stinging anguish. I, on the other hand, remained consoled. Although Mama was taken, still, we had you. Naive though it may seem, I appeared as a child, deprived of a favorite toy, but quickly given another. Although the child, most likely adapts, should there be no substitute, screams of rage would soon fill the air.

Sometimes, when alone, my cries pierce the stone wall of agony. I sob, tormented by the realization that the most for which we can hope, is the warmth of your spirits as they fill the halls where we perform.

Indeed, your spirits enjoined our hearts last evening, as Harry sang a song dedicated to your memory. The depth of longing and despair heightened, somehow, reaching Harry's voice and my fingertips at the piano. We knew you and Mama were there, but oh, how I ached for your physical presence.

Once again, I saw myself as a young girl, appearing at the annual recital held each spring in the institute. I felt captivating in the lush, chocolate brown cotton dress, with bib yoke of eyelet, ruffled to the waist. Each year, at recital time, Mama and I went shopping. Invariably, a new outfit indicated a special, *very* special occasion; and not of frivolous account.

Towards the end of the recital, I shyly stepped to the front of the long, dual parlor, where there stood a concert grand piano. Recitals provided one with a good rule of thumb for measuring progress. We knew, instantly, how well we fared, simply by noting our name on the program. This year, I was second from last. Durst I steal a casual glance at the audience before commencing? Arranging my skirt on the leather piano bench, I peered sidewise at the sea of faces in the audience.

Our eyes met. In proud anticipation, you and Mama sat on the edges of your seats. We exchanged smiles and I felt reassured. Thus, it was during several decades. I truly believe the greatest pleasure experienced during your lives, was merited by your attendance at musicales, recitals and concerts in which we participated.

You and Mama were our most ardent admirers. In the highly competitive music world, I felt secure and rewarded by your pleasure and confidence. No matter what the petty grievances amongst professional colleagues, you were there, encouraging us to pleasurable eminence, felt with sense of achievement.

Now, our performance is void of the pureness of love sustained when you sat in the audience. Admirers continue to patronize our appearance each season. They are warm, faithful and captivated concertgoers. Still, I search, face after face, in desperate endeavor to discern your smiling countenance in the audience. There persists a feeling of quiet desperation. I know now, that it will be so the rest of my life.

Rabbi Lazer

"Who is like unto thee, O Lord, among the gods? who is like thee, glorious in holiness, fearful in praises, doing wonders?"
Exodus 15:11

Dearest Daddy,

Surrounded by the stillness of early morning, I pause to reflect upon the subtle transformation of our lives during the past few months. This morning at 7:00 a.m., Sherri's plane left for Crown Heights. I sense the twinkle in your eye as you muse, *"Crown Heights? Why is my twenty-two year old granddaughter traveling to that secluded mecca of Chasidic Jewry? One of few communities where the pious brethren remaining amongst our people still observe the traditions of our heritage. A wedding? Whom could she possibly know in Crown Heights?"*

During the past half century, family members migrated from the burroughs of New York to small towns and cities upstate. Gradually, witnessing the erosion of many intricate observances, one had to be reminded of their existence. A trip to Crown Heights was a supreme manner in which to awaken the mind.

Oftentimes, during our childhood and even in later years, you enjoyed referring to Buba and Zeda, your parents, by that endearing phrase, *Zawl zain a gute beter für uns*.

"What does that mean, Daddy?" I inquired while still a young girl.

"Well, honey," you began. *"It means that when someone you love dies, and the soul reaches upward to the heavens, that person serves as a spokesman for the dear ones left behind here on earth. In other words, he can put in a good word or two with 'der Eibihshter, the Most*

High,' in order to facilitate our lives."

Frequently, after your departure, I experienced the customary feeling of having been forsaken. Nothing, and no one, can ever compensate for the sensation of abandonment experienced when we lose a loved one. Surely, not for the loss of a parent, brother, sister or child. Yet, we are compelled to continue with our daily lives, or succumb to despair.

Suddenly, one day a few months later, a tall, solemn figure appeared at our front door.

"Mrs. Stein?" he questioned in a quiet voice.

"Yes," I replied in dubious intonation.

"I'm Rabbi Lazer. Your friend, Hal Rosen, asked me to see you. I understand you're interested in promoting traditional observance in this area."

Struck by the awesome figure, I invited him to enter. His elevated stature was offset by rounded shoulders and a full, dark beard, obviously allowed resolute nurture for many years. His dark eyes behind spectacles, stared in a combination of half-smiling solemnity.

Quickly, I tried to recall certain ideas you and I had frequently discussed. Even as your strength ebbed, you never lost hope that the methodical erosion of our traditions would reverse. That somehow, someone, somewhere, would come into our midst and answer the plea for help. So much had transpired during that last decade, always subtle, forever proclaimed in the name of progress. Living in an area where few associates knew one tradition from another, and even less numbers cared, we witnessed a steadfast, morose decay of the heritage respected by our grandparents at the turn of the century.

Zawl zein a gute beter für uns. In that very instant, I knew why Rabbi Lazer was sitting in our dining room. Inwardly, I squealed for joy. The hidden delight rebelliously surfaced and resulted in uncontrollable tears.

"*I don't know why I'm crying,*" I blubbered to the Rabbi.

"*You're crying because you care,*" came a quiet response. "*You care about our people and what will become of the next generation. Where are we headed? Who is going to stop this influx of new and modern ideas? The turmoil and denial of spiritual grace once bestowed upon generation after generation?*"

And so it began. Conversation after conversation with Rabbi Lazer. Rabbi Lazer, whose beautiful, angelic wife, Rebbetzin Devorah, lived with their seven children in Canada, was the spiritual traveling salesman of the south. Many were the nicknames he acquired from those whose homes he frequented. The traveling Rabbi, the flying Rabbi, the Rabbi with wings, the Rabbi of countless good deeds.

"*How does he do it?*" we queried one another. "*His wife must be an angel.*"

"*My wife 'is' an angel,*" he'd often reply. "*How else could I manage?*"

Wonder upon wonder, this remarkable spiritual leader accomplished. Frequently, on an early Monday morning, the telephone would ring.

"*Hello, Rabbi Lazer. From where are you calling?*"

Answers ranged from the deep throes of the south to frigid horizons of the faraway north. Quickly, we became accustomed to the weekly visits and phone calls. His indefatigable desire to help rejuvenate the faith of those who had exchanged spirituality for sunny days in the tropics, manifested itself in countless instances. His knowledge of tradition and persistent adherence to detail, were as splendid music to our hungering souls.

How long had it been since we had gloried in the

sights and sounds that beckoned to the roots of our heritage? The years had been filled with what leaders blindly referred to as progress. Progressive insights were the order of the day.

We must change with the times, an oft quoted challenge. *We must listen to our youngsters and their cries of need.* Ah, yes, but take another look at this bearded figure. Something shines from within; a warmth from which progressive leaders flee in panic.

"Too old-fashioned!" they scream. And with them, the stampede of sheep they guide.

But a few of us come forth. We remove ourselves from the cries and condemnations.

The glib remarks are volunteered in rapid succession as we calmly proceed with our endeavor. Only *we* realize how much richer our lives have become, in spite of those who wilfully seek to destroy. And *I, alone,* possess the secret of whence Rabbi Lazer came. *Zawl zein a gute beter für uns.* Our prayers have been answered.

Dreams

*"In the Lord shall all
the seed of Israel
Be justified, and shall
glory."*
Isiah 45:25

Dearest Daddy,

At the end of a narrow alcove, approaching the hotel conference room, we stood together. You were wearing a dark gray suit, white shirt and paisley necktie. A friend had once reminisced, *"Even your Dad looked the same to me. I always remember him dressed up with a tie."* The feelings were powerful as I anxiously scrutinized your behavior.

Something soft and strange as an invisible blanket had come over you. In a subtle manner, you seemed to be crying for help. There was nothing precise. Simply innuendos. A weak knee. The sudden, verbal lament, that you wished Mama were there. A slight dizziness.

I knew that any suggestion of a plea for help, or a trip to the hospital, would immediately thrust our relationship into jeopardy. Once again, we must see it through ourselves. Fear, probably stemming from previous involvements, had long ago resulted in viewing medical assistance as a last resort.

Suddenly, you descended to your knees, hands sinking into the thick carpet. Feelings of desperation enveloped me as I attempted to help. Quickly dismissing ideas of a serious nature, you explained that a weak leg must have given way. We continued to converse with the few stragglers nearby. At this point, I was not even certain as to the nature of our meeting. Only the room, you, and I, seemed terribly real. A friend appeared to be at the other end of the alcove, awaiting our departure.

With one arm, I held you tightly as, with the other, I struggled to maintain balance. Feelings of desperation and despair were mingled with intense happiness at your simply being there to attend.

I began to cry. Tears flowed in release as my eyes opened. Staring up at the bedroom ceiling, I was seized by a sudden emptiness. The reality of morning. Another day.

Epilogue

"I will sing unto the Lord, because he hath dealt bountifully with me."
Psalms 13:7

Dearest Daddy,

A decade has passed since Mama's death and more than eight years since your departure from the family circle. Your nine grandchildren have developed into fine young men and women of whom you and Mama would be justly proud. Amongst the brood, there exists a stimulating diversity of business enterprise, professionalism, collegiate achievement and reverential ideals.

During the past few years, there has been an influx of young adults who have become *Bal t' shuva* or returnees to the practice of Judaism in its absolute adherence, that was the custom of our great-grandparents and your parents. Several of your grandchildren have assumed this role, much to the credit of you and Mama and the ideals you portrayed during your lifetime. These young adults, with their noble endeavors, have had an intense effect on our lives and have served to elevate our standards and sustain our heritage. Along with your other grandchildren, they continue to provide joy and satisfaction within our daily lives.

Once again, Daddy, we are in the midst of the High Holy Day season, a time to gain perspective and enhanced spirituality. We remember now, those words spoken by you and Mama each year, especially during these Days of Awe. *We have much for which to be thankful*. Eight small words that evoke indelible mental images of you and Mama, two lives that made a difference.

Glossary

The following glossary provides an explanation of the Hebrew or Yiddish words and phrases used in this book. Often, there are alternate spellings and meanings for the words.

BAR MITZVAH: Literally, *son of the commandment* referring to a Jewish boy, aged thirteen, who is obligated to assume his place as an adult member of the Jewish religious community. The celebration of this occasion, after which TEFILLIN are put on every weekday morning and he is counted as one of the ten necessary for a MINYAN.

BAS, BAT: daughter of

BAS or BAT MITZVAH: Literally, *daughter of the commandment* female equivalent of Bar Mitzvah. Ceremony, usually at age twelve, (but sometimes done at thirteen), inducting a Jewish girl into the fold. According to Orthodox tradition, Jewish women do not wear TEFILLIN and are not counted as part of a MINYAN.

BEN: son of

BIMAH: Platform or dais; the raised platform from which the TORAH is read in the synagogue.

BLECH: tin. A sheet of tin kept on the stove, over a warm burner, to keep food warm on the Sabbath, since creation of a flame or electrical convenience is forbidden.

BRIHT MILA: also spelled Brihs Milaw, Brit Mila. Literally, *covenant of circumcision*. A ritual circumcision performed on the eighth day after the birth of a Jewish boy, in which the child becomes a part of the Jewish people.

BRISS: also Brihs, Briht, Brit, Bris, Berit. Abbreviated form of BRIHT MILA.

BUBA: also Buhbuh, Bawbe, Buhbe, Bube, Bubbe. Grandmother.

CANTOR: also referred to as Chazn, Chazan, Hazan, Chazzen, Hazzan. One who leads the congregation of a synagogue in the songs and performs liturgical solos. The Cantor usually prepares students for Bar and Bat Mitzvah. Most Conservative Temples and many Reform, Orthodox or Reconstructionist congregations, employ both a Rabbi and a Cantor.

CHALA: also Chaluh, Chale, Cha-law, Challah. The traditional loaf of rich, white bread, usually braided or twisted, eaten by Jewish people on the Sabbath and holidays, except for Passover, when only unleavened bread or Matzoh must be eaten.

CHANUKAH: also spelled Chanuka, Hanukah, Hanuka, Hannuka. A Jewish holiday that usually falls in the month of December (having absolutely nothing in common with Christmas, but too often, associated with that holiday) commemorating victory of the Maccabees in 165 B.C.E. over the Syrian-Greek rulers of Palestine in a struggle for their religious freedom. Celebrated as an eight day festival beginning with the twenty-fifth day of the Hebrew month Kislev.

CHASID, CHASSIDIC: pl. CHASIDIM. A pious person. A follower of the eighteenth century Israel Baal Shem Tov in Eastern Europe. Emphasis on strict tradition.

CHEDER: also spelled cheidr, heder. A room. An elementary Jewish school where basic traditions, reading of Hebrew is taught. Usually, wherein the Jewish student attends classes several days weekly, after public school hours. There is a trend whereby Jewish day schools eliminate the necessity for a Cheder in some communities.

CHOLENT: also spelled Chawlent. A Sabbath dish of meat, beans, peas, and other ingredients cooked before sunset on Friday and kept hot to be eaten on Saturday, thus avoiding violation of the Sabbath by cooking.

CHUPUH: also spelled Chupe, Choopa, Choopaw, Choope, Huppa. A bridal canopy, under which the bride and groom, and usually close relatives, especially parents, stand for the wedding ceremony.

CONSERVATIVE: A movement in Judaism that accepts moderate adaptation of religious ritual, allowing men and women to sit together during services, and practice of less strict adherance than Orthodox.

DAVEN, DAVENEN: also Davn, Davnen. To pray. To recite the prayers of daily or holiday liturgy. Usually read in Hebrew, and often at a rapid pace by steady adherents.

DREIDL: also spelled Draydl, Dreidel, Dredel. A four-sided top used on the Chanukah holiday. Each side has a Hebrew letter enabling players to keep score for the game played by spinning the top. Dreidls come in many colors, sizes and materials, such as plastic or wood.

EIBIHSHTER: (der). Also der Ihbershter. Literally, *the Most High* or God.

EREV: Evening. The eve of a holy day. All Jewish holy days begin on the evening before the designated date, at sundown.

FLAISHIG: also spelled, Fleishihg, Fleishihk, Flaishig, Flaishik. Meat or meat products as well as utensils that have been used in preparation or serving of meat products. In contrast to MILCHIG.

GROGGER: also spelled Gragr, Grager. A noisemaker used in the synagogue on the PURIM holiday during the reading of the MEGILLA, to denigrate the name of HAMAN whenever it is mentioned.

HAFTORAH: also spelled Haftarah, Haftara. A selection from the books of the Hebrew Prophets which follows the reading of the Pentateuch in synagogues on the Sabbath and holidays. The prophetic portion read by the BAR MITZVAH and the BAT MITZVAH.

HAGGADAH: also spelled Hagada, Haggada. Literally *the telling, narration* contained in the Passover SEDER prayerbook, in which the story of the Exodus is told. Used at the family celebrations on the first two nights of Passover.

HA KOHEN: the priest. A descendant of a priestly family. A designated title handed down from father to son, generation to generation, dating back to biblical history. A Jewish person may be the son or daughter of one of three designated titles - Kohen, Levi or Israelite. Each is given different honors during the service, Kohen the highest.

HAK MIHR NIHT IHN KUHP: Literally, *Stop chopping at my head*. Stop annoying me!

HALEIVI: Often pronounced a-le-vai. Also spelled halevai. Perhaps. May it only happen!

HAMAN: the villain in the Book of Esther, recited during the holiday of PURIM.

HAMANTASH: A triangular pastry filled with poppy seeds, prunes, or cheese and eaten on PURIM; named after HAMAN, the Purim villain. pl. HAMANTASHEN.

HASHEM: also Ha-Sheim. Literally, *the (Divine) Name* God, used as a substitute for Adonai.

HIGH HOLY DAYS: the period encompassing ROSH HASHONAH and YOM KIPPUR in the Jewish Calendar. Each year, these days fall sometime during the months of September and October.

KADDISH: also spelled Kadihsh. Literally, *sanctification*. The Mourner's Prayer recited several times during the service. Following the loss of a parent, child, brother, sister or spouse, men are obligated and women may recite this prayer during eleven months of regular attendance at synagogue. Kaddish is also recited at various times during the service, as a non-mournful prayer.

KIDDUSH: also spelled Kihdoosh. Literally, *sanctification*. The blessing recited over wine on the Sabbath and holidays.

KNEIDL: also spelled knaydl, knaidel, knaidle, knaidl. pl. kneidlach and knaidlach. A dumpling, usually made with matza meal, eggs, water and chicken fat, or various substitutes. Served in chicken soup, especially on Passover or other holidays and Sabbath.

KOHEN: see HA KOHEN.

KOSHER: also KASHRUT, KASHER, KASHRUT, KASHRUTH. The state of being in accordance with Jewish dietary laws as specified in Leviticus 11 and elaborated upon in the TALMUD and later codes of law. Clean or fit to eat according to these laws. Serving or dealing with such food, such as in a kosher kitchen. Strict supervision by a Rabbi or other designated individual is required by Jewish law.

KUGEL: also spelled kugl, koogel. A pudding, sweet or savory, usually made with noodles or potatoes.

LOKSHEN KUGEL: also spelled luhkshn kugl, lukshen kugel. Noodle pudding.

MAVEN: also spelled meivihn, maivin. Expert. Authority. Connoisseur.

MEGILLA: also megihle, megilaw, megihluh, megila. Literally, *scroll*. A generic name of five biblical books: Esther, Ecclesiastes, Song of Songs, Ruth, and Lamentations. "The Megilla" is the book of Esther, read on PURIM.

MILCHIG: also spelled milchik, mihlchihk, also said as milchedik. Dairy products as well as utensils that have been used in preparation or serving of dairy products. In contrast to FLAISHIG.

MINYAN: pl. MINYANIM. Also spelled mihnyan, mihnyawn, minyon. Literally, *count*. A quorum of ten (traditionally male, but recently considered by some movements, to include female) Jews, over the age of thirteen, required for communal worship.

MOHEL: also spelled Moil, Moheil, Mohayl. A person trained to perform circumcisions according to Jewish law. Often, a specially trained Rabbi or Cantor.

MOURNER'S KADDISH: see KADDISH.

NACHES: also spelled nachuhs, nachas, nachat. Pride. Satisfaction from another's achievement. Often used as parent achieving from child.

OIF MEINE SONIM GEZAWGT: Literally, *(such a fate) should be said about my enemies. May my enemies have my fate!*

ONEG SHABAT: also Oneg Shabuhs, Oineg Shabes, Oneg Shabbat. Literally, *delight of the Sabbath*. A celebration held on Friday night to honor the Sabbath.

ORTHODOX: strictly conforming to the rites and traditions of Judaism, such as Kashrut, Sabbath, etc. as formulated by the Torah and Talmud.

PAREVE: also spelled parev. Food products that are neither dairy nor meat, including fruit, vegetables, fish, and all meatless and synthetic products.

PASSOVER: Literally, *to pass over*. The Festival of Freedom that commemorates the deliverance of the ancient Hebrews from slavery in Egypt. Observed by worldwide Jewry for eight days, except seven days in Israel. Special dietary laws prevail, food strictly KOSHER for Passover; Matzoh, the unleavened bread, eaten throughout the holiday.

PESACH: also spelled Peisuhch, Pesah. See Passover.

PHYLACTERIES: translation for TEFILLIN. See TEFILLIN.

PURIM: also spelled Poorihm. A holiday celebrated on the fourteenth day of the Hebrew month Adar, usually during the month of March, Purim marks the deliverance of the Jews of ancient Persia from HAMAN's plot to exterminate them, as recorded in the biblical Book (Scroll) of Esther.

PUST: Idle. Lack of activity.

RABBI: Teacher. Master. A scholar and teacher of Jewish law. Usually, the spiritual head of a congregation, qualified to decide questions of law and ritual and to perform marriages.

REBBE: Rabbi. Teacher. Usually, a highly venerated spiritual leader or teacher, especially of a Chasidic sect.

REBBETZIN: the wife of a Rabbi.

REFORM: A movement in Judaism that seeks to stress rational thought with historical belief, stressing its ethical aspects without strict observance of traditional Orthodox or Conservative ritual.

ROSH HASHONAH: also spelled Rosh Hashona. Literally, *the head (beginning) of the year*. The Jewish New Year, celebrated on the first and second days of the Hebrew month Tishrei, usually occurring during September and/or October. Observed for both days by Orthodox and Conservative Jews; one day by Reform Jews.

SEDER: also Seidr. Literally, *order, arrangement*. PASSOVER service and elaborate meal during which the HAGGADAH is read. Most traditional Jews conduct a Seder for the first two nights of Passover.

SEDER PLATE: A specially designed plate containing indentations or separate small dishes, in which various foods, symbolic of the PASSOVER holiday are placed. This symbolic plate and its contents, are an integral part of the SEDER.

SHABAT: also Shabbos, Shabuhs, Shabes, Shabbes. Literally, *rest*. The Sabbath day, a day of rest.

SHTETL: also spelled shtetel. A small town, particularly in the Jewish communities of Eastern Europe.

SHUL: Literally, *school*. Synagogue.

SIDDUR: also spelled Sihdr, Sidoor. Literally, *arrangement, order*. Prayerbook with the daily, Sabbath or Festival liturgies.

SIMCHA: also spelled sihmchuh, sihmcha, simche, simha. Joy, rejoicing. A festive celebration.

SIMCHAT TORAH: also spelled Sihmchas Toruh. Literally, *rejoicing in the law*. The festival after SUCCOTH, marking both the completion and beginning of the annual cycle of TORAH readings in the synagogue.

SUCCAH: also spelled sukaw, sukuh, sukkah. A booth covered with branches, constructed for the festival of SUCCOTH, to commemorate booths lived in by Israelites during their wanderings after the Exodus from Egypt. Many Jews of the Orthodox, Conservative or Reform movements, build their own edifice, elaborately decorated by children or adults, and eat their main meals therein, during the holiday.

SUCCOTH: also spelled Sukos, Sukot, Sukkot. Literally, *booths*. The eight day festival marking the fall harvest and the wandering of the Israelites in the wilderness of Sinai en route to the Promised Land following the Exodus from Egypt.

SYNAGOGUE: a bringing together; an assembly of Jews brought together for worship and religious study. A building or place used by Jewish people for that purpose.

TALLIT: also spelled taliht, tallis, talith, talis, talit. A rectangular prayer shawl with fringes on each corner, worn by some, large enough to cover the entire back; by others, surrounding the shoulders. Some prefer at times during the service in more observant movements, to raise the Tallit, so that it also covers the head, allowing for privacy during prayer.

TALMUD, TALMUDIC: the collection of writings constituting the Jewish civil and religious law. It consists of two parts, the Mishna (text) and the Gemara (community). Literally, *study, learning*. The compendium of discussions and interpretations of the biblical text by the scholars of Palestine and Babylonia from 500 B.C. to 500 C.E.

TANTE: also spelled tantuh. Aunt

TEFILLIN: two black leather boxes containing TORAH verses, which are bound by black leather straps, to the arm and head of adult males during morning prayers, except on SHABAT and Holy Days. PHYLACTERIES.

TORAH: Teaching. The Law. A parchment scroll containing the Pentateuch, the first five books of the Bible. The whole body of Jewish religious literature.

TSIHMES: also spelled tsimmes, tzimmes. A compote, usually of cooked fruit, and/or vegetables such as potatoes, carrots, prunes or plums.

VUHS HAKST DU MIHR IHN KUHP? Literally, *For what are you chopping my head off?* Why are you talking me to death?

YAHRZEIT: also spelled yartsait, yartzeit, yortzeit, yohrtzeit. Literally, *year's time*. The anniversary of a death, observed by lighting a special candle or electric memorial light for twenty-four hours.

YARMULKE: also spelled yarmulka, yamulke, yarmuhlke. A skullcap worn by Orthodox and Conservative Jewish men at prayer, and at all times by observant Orthodox males.

YIDDISH: also spelled Yihdihsh. Literally, *Jewish*. The mother-tongue of Ashkenazic (East European) Jews and their descendants in other countries, derived from approximately 75 per cent medieval High German and 25 percent Hebrew and written in Hebrew letters.

YIZKOR: Literally, *remember*. A Memorial service held on the last day of Passover, the second day of Shevuot, on Yom Kippur and on Shemini Atzereth, conclusion of the SUCCOTH Festival.

YOM KIPPUR: also spelled Yom Kihpr. Literally, *Day of Atonement* observed on the tenth day of Tishri on the Hebrew calendar. A day of fasting and solemn prayer.

ZEDA: also spelled Zaide, Zeide, Zayde, Zeiduh. Grandfather.

THE OLIVE TREE

ARLENE C. STEIN

ARLENE C. STEIN

S.I.M.A. PUBLISHERS
P.O. Box 25423
Tamarac, FL 33320-5423

Please send _____ copies of
The Olive Tree at $18.00. Please add $2.00
to cover postage & handling.

NAME _____

ADDRESS _____

CITY _____ STATE _____ ZIP _____

Check enclosed _____
Please make payable to: Arlene C. Stein